The Three Secrets
of Green Business

The Three Secrets of Green Business

Unlocking Competitive Advantage
in a Low Carbon Economy

GARETH KANE

publishing for a sustainable future

London • Sterling, VA

First published by Earthscan in the UK and USA in 2010

HB ISBN: 978–1-84407–873–8
PB ISBN: 978–1-84407–874–5

Typeset by Saxon Graphics Ltd, Derby
Cover design by Rob Watts

For a full list of publications please contact:

Earthscan
Dunstan House
14a St Cross St
London, EC1N 8XA, UK
Tel: +44 (0)20 7841 1930
Fax: +44 (0)20 7242 1474
Email: earthinfo@earthscan.co.uk
Web: **www.earthscan.co.uk**

22883 Quicksilver Drive, Sterling, VA 20166–2012, USA

Earthscan publishes in association with the International Institute for Environment and Development

A catalogue record for this book is available from the British Library

Library of Congress Cataloging-in-Publication Data

Kane, Gareth.
    The three secrets of green business : unlocking competitive advantage in a low carbon economy / Gareth Kane.
        p. cm.
    Includes index.
    ISBN 978-1-84407-873-8 (hardback) – ISBN 978-1-84407-874-5 (pbk.) 1. Business enterprises-
Environmental aspects. 2. Management-Environmental aspects. 3. Green products. I. Title.
    HD30.255.K357 2009
    658.4′083-dc22

                                        2009021283

At Earthscan we strive to minimize our environmental impacts and
carbon footprint through reducing waste, recycling and offsetting our
CO_2 emissions, including those created through publication of this
book. For more details of our environmental policy, see
www.earthscan.co.uk.

This book was printed in the UK by TJ International, an ISO 14001
accredited company. The paper used is FSC certified and the inks are
vegetable based.

For Harry
and his generation

Contents

List of Figures, Tables and Boxes

Figures

Tables

Boxes

About the Author

Gareth Kane was born and brought up in Northern Ireland before moving to England to study engineering at Christ's College, Cambridge in the early 1990s. It was at college that he made his first steps down the environmental path, becoming a founding member of the Green Society and getting elected to the Student Union as Green Officer where he implemented a recycling system embedded into college life.

A couple of years after graduating, he found himself teaching English in Murmansk in the far north of Russia. A trip to nearby Monchegorsk was his first experience of massive ecological destruction – acid rain caused by the town's nickel smelter had wiped out life on the tundra for miles around. There and then he decided that his calling in life was to prevent such environmental damage.

On return to the UK he joined the 'Design for a Clean Environment' project at Newcastle University where he learned much of the theory behind the principles put forward in this book. He also gained an MPhil in the eco-design of large products such as ships and oil platforms.

His next move was to lead the new Clean Environment Management Centre (CLEMANCE) at the University of Teesside. Here he put the theory into practice, working with over 200 companies to improve their environmental performance. His biggest achievement was conceiving, planning and implementing the Tees Valley Industrial Symbiosis Project (TVISP). This was, and still is, one of the biggest environmental projects in the country, diverting over 150,000 tonnes of 'waste' away from landfill and into practical uses. The principles of Industrial Symbiosis (IS) are outlined in Chapter 5.

In 2004 Gareth was elected as a member of Newcastle City Council where he is Executive Support Member for Climate Change and Sustainability, a member of the Environmental & Sustainability Policy Group, sponsor of the Local Authority Carbon Management Programme and represents the council in a number of partnerships including the Newcastle Warm Zone, Newcastle Groundwork Partnership, the Association of North East Councils Climate

Change Task Group and Carbon Neutral North East. He put forward a motion to council to sign the Nottingham Declaration on Climate Change, triggering the development of a Climate Change Strategy.

In 2006 Gareth left CLEMANCE to set up a new business, Terra Infirma Ltd (www.terrainfirma.co.uk), which provides cutting-edge support to businesses to help them improve their environmental performance and their bottom line. Clients include the Department for Environment, Food and Rural Affairs (DEFRA) Sustainable Consumption and Production Programme, Envirowise, the European Union, Gentoo Housing Group, Stone Homes Ltd, Durham County Council and numerous others. He also comments on environmental issues for a number of websites, not least his own Sustainable Business Blog (www.terrainfirma.co.uk/blog.html) and Eco-living Blog (http://eco-living.blogspot.com).

Gareth has appeared as a media pundit on sustainability issues on the BBC 'Six O'Clock News', 'Countryfile' and 'The Politics Show'. In 2008 he was named as a 'Rising Star, Future Leader' by *The Journal* newspaper for his work on sustainability. He lives in Newcastle upon Tyne with his partner Karen, sons Harry and Jimmy, and Pip the Cat.

Acknowledgements

I would like to acknowledge all those who have helped me through the years: my colleagues at Newcastle University and CLEMANCE and all my clients and project partners at Terra Infirma.

I must thank Lorenzo Wood of LBi UK and Dr Karen Johnson of Durham University for proofreading my manuscript and providing editorial suggestions. Thanks must also go to the staff at Earthscan, in particular Rob West, Camille Bramall and Dan Harding, for their hard work, expertise and, most of all, patience.

This book would not have been written without the support of my family: Karen, Harry, Jimmy and Pip.

List of Acronyms and Abbreviations

ASA	Advertising Standards Agency
BOD/COD	Biological/Chemical Oxygen Demand
BRE	Building Research Establishment
BREEAM	BRE Environmental Assessment Method
CCS	Carbon Capture and Storage
CDM	Clean Development Mechanism
CFCs	chlorofluorocarbons
CFL	Compact Fluorescent Light
CLEMANCE	Clean Environment Management Centre
COD	Chemical Oxygen Demand
CoP	Coefficient of Performance
CSR	Corporate Social Responsibility
DEFRA	Department for Environment, Food and Rural Affairs
DETR	Department of the Environment, Transport and the Regions
DfT	Department for Transport
EMAS	Environmental Management and Audit System
EMS	Environmental Management System
FMCEA	Failure Mode Cause & Effect Analysis
FSC	Forest Stewardship Council
FTA	Fault Tree Analysis
GIS	Graphical Information System
GM	genetically modified
GSHP	Ground Source Heat Pumps
HAZOP	Hazard and Operability
HFCs	hydrofluorocarbons
HVAC	Heating, Ventilation and/or Air Conditioning
IEMA	Institute of Environmental Management and Assessment
IPC	Integrated Pollution Control
IPPC	Integrated Pollution Prevention and Control

IS	Industrial Symbiosis
ISIE	International Society for Industrial Ecology
KPIs	Key Performance Indicators
LCA	Life Cycle Assessment
LEED	Leadership in Energy and Environmental Design
MJ	megajoule
MPG	miles per gallon
MSC	Marine Stewardship Council
NDAs	Non-Disclosure Agreements
NGO	non-governmental organization
NIMBY	Not In My Back Yard
NISP	National Industrial Symbiosis Programme
PFCs	perfluorocarbons
PV	photovoltaic
ROCs	Renewable Obligation Certificates
SS	Suspended Solids
SUDS	Sustainable Urban Drainage Systems
TNS	The Natural Step
TQM	Total Quality Management
TVISP	Tees Valley Industrial Symbiosis Project
W	watt
WEEE	Waste Electrical and Electronic Equipment
WRAP	Waste Resources Action Programme
WWF	World Wide Fund for Nature
WYGIWYN	What You Get Is What You Need

Introduction

Why write this book?

At the time of writing I have spent over a decade helping hundreds of businesses, public sector and not-for profit organizations to transform the environmental impact of their activities.

It has taken me all those years to accumulate all this knowledge and experience: there is no book or other publication that will take the reader through the practical process of delivering sustainability in a 'how to' manner. There is plenty of advice out there on environmental management (Chapter 3) and the 'small steps' that a company can take (Chapter 4), but it takes a lot of time to pull it all together. There are many books that debate the theory and examples of some of the 'huge leaps' described in Chapter 5, but nothing that knits them all together. What this book does for the first time is give you a practical roadmap from here to sustainability. The examples and tips in this book have been drawn from practical experience – they work.

How to use this book

This book is structured into five chapters:

- Chapter 1 Setting the Scene;
- Chapter 2 The Three Secrets of Green Business Success;
- Chapter 3 Preparing to Go Green: the groundwork required to make change happen in your organization;
- Chapter 4 Small Steps: the basic steps you should undertake to make your business leaner and greener;
- Chapter 5 Huge Leaps: the higher risk, higher reward strategies you can take to move towards a truly sustainable business.

If you want a truly green business, then you will need to read all five chapters in order. If you are simply looking for incremental improvements to your environmental performance then you will find Chapter 4 a useful reference guide, however you may need to refer back to Chapters 1 and 2 occasionally to understand the context.

Chapter 1

Setting the Scene

The Big Picture

A lonely planet

When the crew of Apollo 8 brought back pictures showing the Earth floating like a blue marble in the inky black darkness of space, ripples of consternation were felt across the world. The human race was faced with a stark reality: we live on a finite lump of rock spinning through empty space. Two things had become very clear:

1   Natural resources are not infinite.
2   If we exhaust those resources there is nowhere else to go.

It is important to remember these two basic facts. All too often 'the environment' is discussed in an abstract form as if it is an intangible entity like 'the arts', 'heritage' or 'tradition'. On the contrary, our environment is very real and we can't survive without it.

It is no exaggeration to say that our natural world is in crisis. Climate change has dominated the debate in recent years, but there are plenty of other pressing environmental concerns: the hole in the ozone layer, acid rain, accumulation of toxins in the food chain, loss of biodiversity, loss of topsoil, pollution of seas, lakes and rivers and the unsustainable exploitation of renewable, but depletable, resources such as forests, fish stocks and fresh water.

The facts are staggering. If the population of the whole world were to live like citizens of the UK, we would need three planets to support that lifestyle. If we all lived like the average US citizen, we'd need five.[1] We only have one. It is only the poverty in which the majority of humankind lives that stops the planet giving up the ghost right now. But with the economies of India and China booming, it is imperative that something is done to make human life on Earth sustainable.

What is an environmental impact?

This is quite a difficult question from a philosophical point of view. Many of our most dramatic landscapes around the world have been shaped by human activity. Identifying what constitutes a negative effect on the natural world is a subjective choice.

From a technical point of view, the following model is generally accepted as the standard definition of an environmental impact. There must be a source of a problem (often the release of a pollutant), a receptor (something to be damaged) and a pathway to connect the two (see Figure 1.1).

This is very simple and it gives us the range of techniques to stop the impact happening – you simply have to remove one of the three components:

- Removing the receptor is the most difficult of the three options and is often impossible. A common example is moving a colony of rare amphibians in the path of a new road. Obviously you can't do this for global environmental problems.
- Removing the pathway means preventing the problem reaching the receptor by a physical barrier (e.g. a filter or an impermeable material) or by transforming the pollutant en route (e.g. by chemical, physical or biological treatment).
- Removing the source removes the problem. In practice this strategy most often works best and costs least. It is the one that will be pursued almost exclusively in this book.

Figure 1.1 The technical definition of an environmental impact

A Sustainable Future

Sustainability and all that

So what end are we trying to achieve? The easy answer is that our existence on this planet should be sustainable – we should arrange our lifestyles so that future generations can continue to flourish. Unfortunately the terms 'sustainability' and 'sustainable development' are often used interchangeably, but there is a clear difference between the two.

Sustainability is the *endpoint* where civilization can thrive within the limits posed by only having one planet. As Jonathon Porritt, the chair of the UK's Sustainable Development Commission, says, 'sustainability is non-negotiable as the opposite of sustainability is extinction'.[2]

Sustainable development is the *process* of getting from here to sustainability (see Figure 1.2). There are many hundreds of definitions of sustainable development, but the most widely accepted, and quoted, definition of sustainable development is that of the Brundtland Commission in 1987:[3]

> Development that meets the needs of the present without compromising the abilities of future generations to meet their own needs.

This, like most definitions of sustainable development, is deliberately vague and is very weak because of that. A more robust definition would be:

> Saving the planet and solving world poverty.

And that's a bit scary.

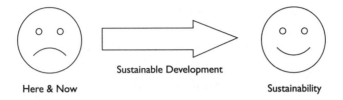

Figure 1.2 Sustainable development and sustainability for dummies

Models of sustainability

The most popular way of visualizing sustainability is three interlocking circles representing economy, society and environment. The nexus at the middle is regarded as sustainability (see Figure 1.3).

While it may sound sensible at first, it is almost entirely useless, if not dangerous, as it suggests that sustainability is some kind of balance between the three and implies that not hitting the target is an option. It is very easy to find a social benefit, an economic benefit and an environmental benefit to any enterprise, but this

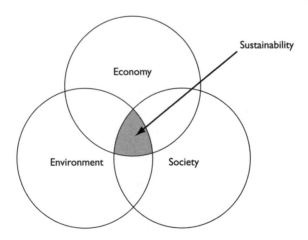

Figure 1.3 Traditional model of sustainability

doesn't mean it is sustainable. To get to true sustainability requires a paradigm shift and that's what we're after in this book.

A slightly more robust version of the interlocking circles is the 'three legged stool' where one leg represents economy, the second is society and the third the environment. The analogy is that if one is removed then the whole thing falls over. While this image gets across the essential services provided by the environment, it is almost impossible to derive any practical policies as a result.

A less well-known but more meaningful model is the 'fried egg' model (see Figure 1.4). In this, sustainability is defined as the situation where the economy operates within the limits set on it by society (which should reflect values such as fairness, justice and liberty), and where society flourishes within the hard ecological limits placed on it by the natural world.

While obviously still high level, this model gives us a more robust objective to aim at. Therefore this is the model I adopt in this book.

This book is predominantly concerned with attaining *environmental* sustainability in industry. Integrating complex social issues into your business, such as human rights and decent working conditions in the supply chain, would require another book to give them the serious consideration they require.

We will consider a number of models of environmental sustainability and how they fit into this high level model in Chapter 2.

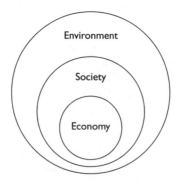

Figure 1.4 'Fried egg' model of sustainability

The Precautionary Principle

Another key plank of sustainable development is the Precautionary Principle. The Precautionary Principle has existed in various forms for several decades and was explicitly included in the Rio Declaration resulting from the first Earth Summit in 1992.

In simple terms the principle states that, given the exceedingly high levels of uncertainty in predicting environmental damage, the prudent approach is to avoid risk and abandon or reject policies or practices that may have unsustainable outcomes or substantial negative environmental impacts.

The Precautionary Principle can be split into six basic concepts:[4]

1   preventative anticipation: protective action should be taken in advance of scientific proof when delay will lead to further environmental damage;
2   safeguarding ecological space: providing suitable margins of error to decrease the probability of unsustainable damage;
3   proportionality of response: these margins of error should be appropriate to the risk involved;
4   duty of care: those who propose change must take responsibility for their actions;
5   promoting natural rights: puts the protection of the environment on a moral as well as practical basis;
6   paying for past ecological debt: puts retrospective liability on polluters and decision-makers.

Environmental legislation is starting to reflect these principles, for example, in the UK:

●   Duty of care is embedded into the waste management regulations. You are responsible for the safe disposal of your waste, no matter who you have contracted to provide this service.
●   Ecological debt: owners of sites with contaminated land can get the people or organization who contaminated that land to pay to clean it up (if they can find them).

Business and the Environment

The environment IS your business

So why should you take the environment seriously when you have a business to run?

The most basic driver is survival. Without the clean air we breathe, the clean water we drink and the materials we require for clothing and shelter, there will be no business, no economy, no nothing.

The next level is the need for business to subsist on a sustainable source of raw materials and energy. Some industries, such as agriculture, horticulture, fisheries and forestry, depend on a sustainable supply of material directly, but all companies require energy and raw materials, even in the service sector.

The highest level is the societal value that human beings put on a clean healthy environment. People pay more for houses with beautiful views, travel around the world to view natural wonders or to lie on clean beaches, and join environmental groups in their millions. Whether they accept it or not, almost everyone is an environmentalist. These people are your customers.

Governments are slowly creaking into action. Hundreds of pieces of legislation are being formulated to drive industry towards sustainability. If industry doesn't move, those inflexible regulations will intensify in number and scope. Many companies are also feeling the heat from the general public as pressure groups launch campaigns on environmental and related issues.

Costs relating to resource use and disposal will rise; both through deliberate introduction of escalating green taxation and through the increasing scarcity of resources. These costs come straight off your bottom line. If you have a 25 per cent profit margin, then for every £1 you spend on environmental costs, you would have to make £4 of sales just to break even. It is almost always easier to cut the cost than increase sales.

On the other hand, a number of trailblazing companies are finding huge commercial advantages to improving environmental performance. Like any

Table 1.1 *Environmental business drivers*

Opportunities	Threats
Reduced costs	Green taxation
More profit	Risk of prosecution
New markets	Customer requirements
Product differentiation	Supply chain pressure
Positive public relations	Negative public relations
Staff morale	NGO campaigns
Future proofing	

situation of change it is better to grasp the nettle and drive forward proactively, seizing the opportunities and leaving the threats far behind. This book sets out a strategy for such a course of action.

Table 1.1 above summarizes environmental business drivers in terms of opportunities and threats.

Industry and the environment

Figure 1.5 shows a simple model of one company. All the arrows in and out represent a cost and an environmental impact. The product or service is the source of income. Obviously the more product you can produce while minimizing the other inputs and outputs, the more profitable the business will be.

Figure 1.6 shows how a large number of companies add up to form a model for the complete product value chain.

Primary industries, which extract resources from the Earth, tend to be the most environmentally destructive. For example, extracting copper ore usually requires the removal of several times as much 'overburden' of soil and rock. Then getting 1kg of pure copper from that ore results in 50–200kg of waste and requires 50–100MJ of energy,[5] enough to light a 100W light bulb for more than ten days. This is the main reason why recycling is important – it cuts out the dirtiest stage of the life cycle.

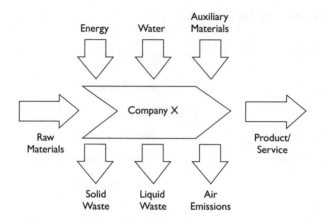

Figure 1.5 One business's impact on the environment

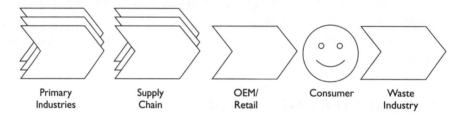

Figure 1.6 The product value chain

The secondary (manufacturing) sector tends to be cleaner and the tertiary sector (retail, services) cleaner still. This provides a problem for companies in the higher levels – if your consumer or client is demanding a more eco-friendly product or service, the main environmental impacts are very likely to be outside your direct control. Conversely, benefits, both economic and environmental, accumulate up the supply chain. If your supply chain is clean and green, then you have to do very little to proclaim yourself clean and green.

Where do we start?

This part of the book has set out the problems that society faces, the endpoint that we must aim for and why this is an issue for your business. But before we get into the practicalities of creating a green business, there are three basic principles that we must understand. Rather grandly, I call these the Three Secrets of Green Business Success.

Chapter 2

The Three Secrets of
Green Business Success

Secret No 1: Understand the Business Case

Secret No 1: Understand the business case

Treat the environmental agenda as an opportunity, not a threat. Grasp it with both hands but, whatever you do, don't forget you are still running a business.

Beyond compliance

Aiming for mere compliance with environmental legislation is a very expensive hobby. If you have an effluent stream containing a certain amount of a toxic material you may have to install a filter or treatment system to reduce its concentration to a legally acceptable level. If the law tightens in the future, you may have to decommission that system and install a more effective alternative. This can and does happen several times over a matter of years, leading to great expense.

If, on the other hand, you design the toxin out of the process, then you will never need to purchase or maintain a treatment system again. This is a key message from this book.

Business opportunities

At the time of writing, UK politicians are desperately trying to outdo each other on the environmental agenda. While they are unlikely to do anything as radical as 'the Governator' – Arnold Schwarzenegger (unsuccessfully) suing major motor manufacturers for billions of dollars of environmental damage – the current situation is a quantum leap forward from recent years, where all the parties thought they were on the cutting edge simply by making their conferences 'carbon neutral'. The focus is shifting too, from the production of goods and services to the other, trickier, side of the equation: consumption. There is finally a realization that an economy in which it is much cheaper to fly from

London to Edinburgh than take the train, will never be sustainable (short of a technological breakthrough on sustainable aviation). To do anything about pressing issues such as climate change, such 'perverse incentives' as the tax breaks on airline fuel will have to be removed.

The general public has traditionally been reluctant to accept responsibility for the impacts of their lifestyle, preferring to point the finger at the authorities or industry. But there is growing evidence in the media that consumers may now be receptive to change and in many cases are actively demanding it.

In the UK, there's been a rash of TV programmes such as 'How Green is Your House', 'No Waste Like Home' and 'It Ain't Easy Being Green'. Quality newspapers such as *The Times, Independent, Guardian* and *Observer* offer regular eco-living columns. Even the notoriously downmarket *Sun* has jumped on the bandwagon. And who would have thought that a film of a legendarily wooden US Vice President giving a PowerPoint presentation would be the documentary hit of the year in 2006?

Out on the high street, evidence of a large-scale shift in spending is also growing. The market share of white goods rated 'A' for energy efficiency rose from 0 per cent in 1996/97 to almost 80 per cent in 2005/06.[6] In the food sector, demand for organic products is far outstripping supply. And DIY giant B&Q is stocking wind turbines and solar panels for domestic use.

The world market for environmental goods and services was valued at US$515 billion in 2000 and was forecast to increase to US$688 billion by 2010. It is anticipated that the next ten years will see even more substantial change.[7]

This nexus of political will and consumer concern has the potential to kick 'green consumerism' out of its niche and into the mainstream, providing an unprecedented business opportunity for both products and services.

And the growing market is a global one. A few years ago I travelled across China by train and saw village after village of modest shacks, each with a brand new shiny solar hot water panel on the roof. If a country of 1.3 billion people wants western standards of living without western levels of pollution, then the markets for green products and services are going to be very big indeed.

Business threats

This book is unashamedly gung-ho about adopting environmental policies as a way to improving your business. But the last thing you should do is forget your business sense.

A green business is *not* a charity.

A green business has to compete with and beat non-green businesses. No-one will feel sorry for you or give you a handout when you need one. I have seen many cases of business people who have caught the green bug and then expected the world to give them a living. For example, I have seen a recycling technology developer almost literally pull his hair out because a local authority wouldn't buy his innovative but highly expensive product. He accused them of stupidity, but I couldn't help thinking that this was a bit rich coming from a so-called businessman who couldn't understand why his target customers weren't buying.

Hitting a consumer wave at the right time has made many people rich, but, unfortunately, the green market has claimed many victims in the past. Too many well-meaning products end up in what US green marketing guru Jacquelyn Ottman calls the 'Green Graveyard',[8] making the fatal assumption that green credentials can overcome mediocre performance, poor design and soppy branding. Successful green products, Ottman argues, look good, perform well and are branded to make clear the benefits of the product to the user rather than the planet.

Other traps face the unwary. For example, in 2002 new rules were introduced in the UK which required all chlorofluorocarbons (CFCs) to be removed from refrigerators before disposal. Removing coolant CFCs was easy as it could simply be drained out, but extracting CFC blowing agents from the fridges' foam insulation was much more difficult. The infamous fridge mountain resulted with fridges being stacked in huge piles in fields. The first companies to import the technology to dispose of fridges in a leak-free manner made a killing. In 2005, the Waste Electrical and Electronic Equipment (WEEE) directive was due to come into law. The directive requires the manufacturers and dealers of such equipment to pay for a certain amount of the equipment they sell to be recycled. Company X, who had joined the fridge-rush slightly late in the day, decided that they would pre-empt the legislation this time and install a WEEE recycling line before the deadline. They were one of very few to do so and stood to profit handsomely. Unfortunately the UK government decided that 'the industry wasn't ready' and, fearing the embarrassment of a white goods mountain once again, delayed the implementation of the directive for 12 months. Company X's line, designed to work three shifts a day, seven days a week, was reduced to running one shift a week for a year, losing substantial sums of money in the process.

This story shows it is imperative not to forget you are running a business and that all the normal rules of commerce apply. In this case it is important not to base a business case around an external factor, such as a political decision, without proper contingency.

Sadly, there is also a small but significant number of sharks out there trying to sell immature or ineffective technologies. This is the case in any economic boom, but the green imperative has provided additional sentimental weak points for the unscrupulous to exploit. I have met several of these crooks in my time and I suggest you keep an eye out. A con man's business is to trick people so be careful: before parting with hard cash, always ask for references (and follow them up), do a credit check and maintain a healthy cynicism.

Your starting point

Existing business

This book assumes that you are in an existing traditional medium to large manufacturing business as this is the worst case scenario for going green. If you are in a different industry (e.g. the service sector) then the manufacturing principles can be used either in your supply chain or with your own clients. Whichever sector you are in, significant change is required, therefore there is a big emphasis in this book on change management (Chapter 3).

Start-ups

Starting up a business is an exhilarating experience. If you are committed to the environment, then to start up a business with strong green credentials is even better. The added bonus is that you do not have a legacy of unsustainable culture, practice and/or capital equipment to change. You start with a blank sheet of paper and you can easily design the principles in Chapters 3, 4 and 5 into your business model.

On the other hand, start-ups need to heed the above advice more than others: you are a business, not a charity. A lack of cash flow will sink you, green intentions or no green intentions. And remember: no sales = no cash = no business. If you haven't already, get some good business advice. I recommend the 'Beermat' series of books by Mike Southon and Chris West.[9] *The Beermat Entrepreneur* will give you an overview of the beermat model (you should be able to write your basic business idea on a beermat) and there are companion books on sales, finance and PR. In the UK, the main organization helping start-ups is Business Link.[10] Some people love them, others loathe them, but I've always found them helpful. Other countries will have their own start-up support organizations.

Social enterprises

It is in fashion to set up green businesses as social enterprises where profits are ploughed into a good cause. While the vast majority of social entrepreneurs do it out of a wider conviction to do the right thing, sadly too many also believe it will make life easy for them. 'Too much social, not enough enterprise' is my rather damning verdict on many such ventures.

The best social enterprise I have seen is the Furniture Resource Centre (FRC) Group which provides a range of services in Liverpool, UK: bulky rubbish collection, furniture recycling and house moving services for the vulnerable. When you go to their offices, a smart receptionist hands out funky visitors' badges which spell out the business's values. Everything is clean, tidy and professional, with nary a hippy in sight. While they charge extra to their clients (in particular Liverpool City Council), they take pains to explain the extra value they bring to the services they offer.

On the other hand, I've seen social enterprises flounder because their prospective clients (usually local authorities) won't deliver a truck full of cash at the mere glimpse of a scrappy business plan. Local authorities are strapped for cash so, if you want them to pay a premium, you'd better offer a premium service – not some vague promise of public 'consultation' and 'engagement'. Again, if your clients aren't buying, it's your fault, not theirs. Social aims, or no social aims, you are still a business.

Is green the new black?

In summary, we're on the cusp of a political and social tipping point where industry must go green or die. Those who surf the green wave to success will be the visionaries who keep their eyes open and their business hats on. The backward-looking will get left behind and the naive will fall by the wayside. So the first secret is:

Treat the environmental agenda as an opportunity, not a threat. Grasp it with both hands but, whatever you do, don't forget you are still running a business.

Secret No 2: What To Do

> ## Secret No 2: What to do
>
> Follow the eco-system model of environmental sustainability or, where you can't, be eco-efficient by a factor of 10.

Environmental strategies

There are broadly two approaches to environmental sustainability:

- eco-efficiency which is largely concerned with *quantities* of materials and energy; and
- eco-system models which are largely concerned with the *type* of materials and energy and *how* we use them.

There is plenty of overlap between the two; however they have quite different implications so we need to explore each in more detail before proceeding.

Eco-efficiency

The theory

Eco-efficiency (also known as 'resource productivity' or 'resource efficiency') is the amount of utility extracted from each unit of natural resource. A good example of an eco-efficiency measure is fuel consumption expressed in miles per gallon (mpg). 'Miles' is the measure of utility and 'gallon' is the unit of resource use.

Eco-efficiency is very business friendly. Utility is what your customers pay for, resources are costs incurred to deliver that function; therefore a company with a high eco-efficiency will tend to be a very profitable company. It is worth noting that efficiency gains are cumulative; in other words lots of incremental improvements in a supply chain can make a final product much more efficient. For example if there are five steps in the supply chain taking a product from raw material to final customer, and all of them manage to reduce their environmental impact by a quarter, then the overall impact of the production of the product will be reduced by more than three quarters.

In 1996, a famous book, *Factor Four: Doubling Wealth, Halving Resource Use*,[11] advocated the use of the eco-efficiency approach to extract twice as much utility from half as many resources, thereby increasing the standard of living while reducing environmental impact. This target has been raised from four to ten by the establishment of the 'Factor Ten Club' of leading environmental thinkers.[12] Factor ten acknowledges that to bring developing countries out of poverty, much bigger efficiency savings are required to account for rising consumption in those countries. Raising the stakes even higher, factor 20 has been mentioned in some quarters.

Examples

There are some good examples of eco-efficiency:

- Compact fluorescent lamps use 15–20 per cent of the energy of incandescent bulbs to produce as much light (factor 5–6).
- The best eco-friendly buildings use less than 10 per cent of the energy of their conventional equivalents (factor 10).
- Air filled bags as protective packaging as opposed to polystyrene chips (at least factor 10).

Problems and issues

Eco-efficiency is a great concept in many ways: simple to understand, reliant on technology and good for business. However, it has a number of problems as described in the following paragraphs.

Technical feasibility

While there are some great examples of high eco-efficiency solutions (see above), many technologies have been more difficult to change. The hybrid-engined

Toyota Prius is regarded as an eco-friendly car, yet it barely outperforms a good diesel car of the same size in fuel efficiency stakes. Airlines will also find it hard, and probably impossible, to come up with fuel efficiency gains in the range of factor 10 and beyond.

The rebound effect

I used to drive a Ford Ka which delivered me to my job 40 miles away reasonably comfortably on a gallon of petrol. After writing the Ka off in a minor accident, I decided to get a diesel VW Golf instead. This did 55mpg, which was great as it cut my fuel consumption by 38 per cent and saved me £250 a year. However this is exactly the cost of a return flight to New York. If I buy the ticket, I've just doubled the amount of carbon dioxide produced while driving the Ka.

This is known as the rebound effect. The example above is an extreme case, but the effect can turn substantial efficiency gains into incremental environmental improvements. Amory Lovins, one of the authors of *Factor Four*, told me that he doesn't believe the effect does exist in reality, but it is implicit in the title of his book – a factor 4 efficiency improvement only leads to a factor 2 reduction in resource use.

Essentially the environmental success of eco-efficiency often depends on consumer/user behaviour which is usually outside your control, unless you radically change the product or service you provide.

False eco-efficiency

It is extremely easy to artificially inflate eco-efficiency figures by choosing your definition of function carefully. I have seen a major computer manufacturer claiming to have improved the eco-efficiency of their laptops by a factor of 7 over five years. On closer inspection, they had used disk and memory capacity as their measure of function. Such parameters are only an intermediate function as far as the user is concerned and their benefits are often mitigated by 'bloatware' – software that has been upgraded so many times that it takes up far more memory and processor time than it should. A more meaningful choice of functionality is required which directly affects the utility provided to the user.

Eco-system models of environmental sustainability

Theory

Take a deep breath. Hold it.

You have just sucked in oxygen, which your body pulls around its systems to release energy from sugars, producing carbon dioxide as a waste product.

OK. Breathe out.

The air is now enriched with that carbon dioxide waste. But this will be recycled back into oxygen and sugars by green leaves using the sun's energy: the miracle that is photosynthesis. All of this is done at concentrations that will not poison you.

Believe it or not, this solar powered, non-toxic closed loop is all you need to know about environmental sustainability. All the Earth's natural systems have functioned in this way for the last billion years, so we can assume that this model is a valid one for humankind to follow to bring us back to sustainability.

Various people have put forward sets of principles so that industry can follow this model. Perhaps the most famous is 'The Natural Step' (TNS),[13] but in my opinion it hides what are essentially simple principles behind jargon and a certain amount of self-importance. I prefer the 'BioThinking'[14] principles put forward by the sustainability consultant Edwin Datchefski as they are stark in their simplicity:

- Solar: all energy is solar;
- Cyclic: all materials move in cycles;
- Safe: the concentrations of all materials are at 'safe' levels.

So, 'Solar, Cyclic, Safe' will be the maxim adopted in the rest of this book. Trips off the tongue, doesn't it? However it can be a little simplistic, so when we want to explore these areas in more detail, I'll call on the work of eco-design gurus William McDonough and Michael Braungart which they call 'Eco-Effectiveness'.[15] Their version of the maxim is:

- Use solar income (as opposed to fossil fuels which are stored solar energy).
- Waste = food: nothing goes to waste, all material flows should be useful or designed out.
- Respect diversity: be compatible with the natural world.

Remember the fried egg model of sustainability? These ecological models define how to operate within the natural limits imposed by a finite planet.

Solar

Anybody who knows their Second Law of Thermodynamics will understand that the world cannot operate indefinitely without an external source of energy. External sources of energy available to us are solar energy and the gravitational pull of the moon, but the latter only affects the tides.

Of course, when we burn fossil fuels, we are using solar energy accumulated by prehistoric plants and stored for millions of years in the Earth's crust, hence McDonough and Braungart's 'Use solar income'. This means we should live off the incoming energy rather than relying on those stores of energy.

We'll look at different forms of renewable energy in Chapter 5.

Cyclic

In nature, there is no such thing as waste. Pretty much everything which is a 'waste' product of one organism becomes food for another part of the system. Oxygen, carbon, nutrients and water all flow in continuous cycles. To mimic these natural cycles, we must begin to cycle all materials in the economy, treating them as resources rather than a disposal issue.

I have a little phrase of my own which I use to help people with this mental leap.

Waste is a verb, not a noun.

The thinking behind this is that by designating a material as 'waste', we are instantly designating it as a problem rather than an opportunity. By using the verb 'waste', we are prejudiced against the *action of wasting* rather than the *resource* itself.

Most of what people call 'recycling' is, strictly speaking, 'downcycling' or the use of materials for a lower purpose than they were first created. An example is the use of food-grade plastic (which is highly regulated for safety) to make park furniture (which could be made of any scrap plastic). Downcycling is not true recycling and simply lengthens the time before the material is of no further use.

'Upcycling' is reusing a material for a higher-grade application than its current use. For example waste platinum from vehicle catalytic converters found in road sweepings can be recycled into jewellery.

For the 'cyclic' requirement to work, all downcycling must be matched by an equivalent amount of upcycling.

McDonough and Braungart introduced the term 'technical nutrients' to describe man-made materials that can be recycled ad infinitum without degradation or substantial pollution, in the same way that biological nutrients are cycled in nature. Certain polymers, glass and metals can all be technical nutrients, provided they are used in the right way.

Safe

One of my favourite eco-anecdotes comes from Gunter Pauli, ex-Chief Executive of Ecover, the eco-friendly domestic product company. He once called a lunchtime press conference to launch his company's new eco-friendly toilet cleaner. All the journalists were served a bowl of salad, but, before they started, Pauli stood up, holding a bottle of his product, and announced he would like to demonstrate how safe the product was. He proceeded to squirt it on his own salad and ate the whole bowl to a stunned silence. This wasn't as foolhardy as it might seem as the product is a mixture of vinegar and palm oils, but it demonstrates that even products for unpleasant jobs such as toilet cleaning can be safe enough to eat.

McDonough and Braungart have a neat little saying: 'Take the filters out of the pipes and put them where they belong – in the designers' heads.'

In other words, don't use toxic materials in the first place. This is a key difference between eco-efficiency and eco-system models. Eco-efficiency doesn't encourage us to substitute materials, merely minimize them. This is a bit like saying 'I'm not murdering as many people as I used to', whereas the eco-system model says 'Thou shalt not kill'.

Examples

There are plenty of good examples of solar-cyclic-safe products and services:

- sheep's wool building insulation;
- sustainably sourced timber products;

- biodiesel fuel made from waste vegetable oil;
- passive biological treatment plants for water.

All of these are natural products or systems but there are fewer examples of 'technical nutrients'.

Problems

The main problem with the eco-system model is that the cycles are limited by our ability to capture the solar energy required to power them. For example in the UK, it is reckoned that there is only enough spare land to produce 5 per cent of the country's fuel demand from biodiesel without impacting on food production.[16] There has been a huge amount of concern about deforestation in Indonesia and other countries for palm oil production to make biodiesel.

Therefore efficiency gains are required in order to make the model feasible. Fortunately, using recycled and natural materials has intrinsic efficiency benefits as their 'embodied energy' (the total energy required to extract, purify and produce material) is usually much lower. For example:

- Recycled aluminium has one-ninth the embodied energy of virgin aluminium.
- Sheep's wool insulation has about one-seventh the embodied energy of mineral wool products.

Therefore switching to the eco-system model will result in reduced energy consumption.

Conclusions

To comply with the 'fried egg' model of sustainability, our endpoint for environmental sustainability must be the eco-system model. However efficiency savings are required as well, particularly in terms of energy, in order to make this model feasible. Hence the second secret:

Follow the eco-system model of environmental sustainability or, where you can't, be eco-efficient by a factor of 10.

Secret No 3: How To Do It

Secret No 3: How to do it

Take some huge leaps *and* lots of small steps.

Most of the environmental improvements I have seen in businesses are incremental – a company will carry out a waste minimization audit or replace a few motors to cut its energy bill. However, given the massive changes required to achieve the sustainability requirements discussed in the previous section, these small steps are never going to deliver on their own.

Types of innovation

When the Sony Walkman appeared in 1979, it revolutionized the way we listened to music. Suddenly we could take our music wherever we went (and annoy the people sitting next to us). As years went by, the Walkman and its copycat rivals were optimized, getting smaller and adding new features. The introduction of the Discman meant that we didn't have to tape our favourite CDs, but could take them with us, and again models got better and better year by year. It was only when MP3 players came along that the music industry was thrown into disarray again. Now it was the music itself that mattered, not the physical means of storing and playing it. Distribution shifted from physical media to electronic data via the internet and users could compile their own playlists of favourite tunes, picking and choosing what they wanted to hear.

The digital revolution has spread to other media as well with RSS feeds allowing internet users effectively to compile their own favourite news and information sources, and blogging has opened up journalism to anyone. As time has gone on, the functionality of these services has gradually improved.

In these examples there are two types of innovation:

- disruptive technologies which change the way we live forever, e.g. the seed drill, the motor car, the internet;
- incremental improvements which ratchet up the performance of those technologies, e.g. faster computer processors, more efficient car engines.

The trick is to do both. Companies who ignore new revolutions will be left behind, but those that make radical changes then sit on their laurels will be overtaken by opportunistic rivals.

Lessons from total quality management

The Total Quality Management (TQM) movement was conceived in the US in the 1950s but took off in Japan, where it has been credited with turning the phrase 'made in Japan' from shorthand for cheap low-quality products into a badge of prestige. The motor industry in particular took it up with a vengeance and ended the dominance of US and European models in the global market, until the west started adopting the same techniques.

TQM describes two types of change:

- *kaikaku*: big radical changes that align a whole system to deliver quality products;
- *kaizen*: continual, incremental improvements within a system to squeeze the best performance out of it.

Kaikaku can be considered as 'doing the right thing' and *kaizen* as 'doing things right'.

I strongly believe that industry should adopt a similar model for environmental performance – big radical changes (like sustainable product development, adopting cleaner manufacturing processes or shifting from a product to a service) should be complemented with basic waste minimization and energy efficiency techniques. If the success of TQM could be replicated in environmental management, we'd be a long way down the road to sustainability.

Sloping staircase model

The result of this is a slightly dangerous looking 'sloping staircase' model consisting of step changes (*kaikaku* or huge leaps) interspaced with continuous incremental improvements (*kaizen* or small steps). Figure 2.1 shows the benefits of this model over simply making incremental improvements.

Each step change on the model requires a radical change of thinking in its own right, overcoming the constraints of the incremental approach. It is essential that each leap upwards takes you up to a 'flexible platform', i.e. one that allows further progress. In other words, one must always plan ahead of the current step to ensure that it does not obstruct further steps towards the ultimate goal of sustainability.

'Cul-de-sacs' are initiatives that, while giving a short-term advantage, eventually lead to a dead end. For example, there is currently much interest in 'clean coal' technologies which use methods such as gasification to produce energy from coal with a fraction of the pollution of standard coal power stations. While this is a significant improvement over the current situation, investment in this technology and its implementation could obstruct truly sustainable renewable energy use in a region for the lifespan of the power station – typically three to five decades.

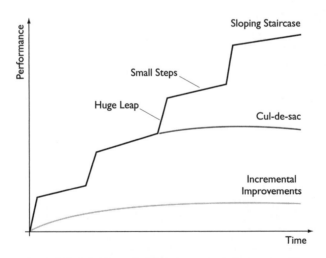

Figure 2.1 Sloping staircase model of innovation

Conclusions

The model proposed applies this idea of two kinds of innovation to environmental performance:

- Small steps (*kaizen*) will drive continual improvement. These are about doing what you do better. Chapter 4 describes a large number of common small steps.
- Huge leaps (*kaikaku*) will realign your business along ecological lines. These are about doing the right thing. Chapter 5 describes the most successful of these strategies.

So the third secret is:

> Take some huge leaps *and* lots of small steps.

But before we do anything we must have the right culture, procedures and strategy to facilitate the radical change as described in this section. This is the purpose of Chapter 3.

Chapter 3

Preparing To Go Green

First things first

The Essentials of Change

Making the change

The magnitude of change required for most businesses either to align to the eco-system model, to deliver a factor 10 improvement in eco-efficiency, or both, is immense. This section provides you with a series of tools and tips to prepare your organization for that change.

Change management theory

Managing change is a huge and complex discipline, but in short, there are two main schools of thought:[17]

- emergent change: the right culture and management direction are created leading to organic movement towards the desired objective;
- planned change: targets are set, projects are planned and implemented, outcomes are measured and monitored.

For sustainability, both approaches are required. A culture of moving in the right direction must be created, but some of the large steps required would not happen without rigorous analysis, planning, implementation and monitoring.

Obstacles to change

Many obstacles stand in the way of change:

- inertia: 'we've always done it this way';
- cynicism: 'just another fad – it'll go the same way as the last one';
- existing capital equipment and facilities: it is usually expensive and physically disruptive to change these;

- immature supply chains: you may find that the materials, technology and sustainable energy you require are in limited supply, expensive, or of poor quality;
- immature markets: as discussed later in this section, some 'green' markets are strong, others non-existent. As we discussed in Secret No 1, you must ensure that your green business offering will be well received by your clients and customers.

The change process

Before you start actually doing anything, you need to:

- make a commitment to change;
- create the *culture* for emergent change to take place;
- develop a *system* for managing planned change and monitoring emergent change: setting targets, creating action plans, resourcing teams and reviewing progress;
- determine a *baseline* for your operations against which to measure progress;
- develop a *vision and strategy* for the future of your organization;
- develop strategy for communicating the results of change to employees, the general public and customers.

This is an iterative process (see Figure 3.1). For clarity the iterations are shown as a neat arrow from monitoring back to strategy, but reality is much messier than this and iterations take place as and when required.

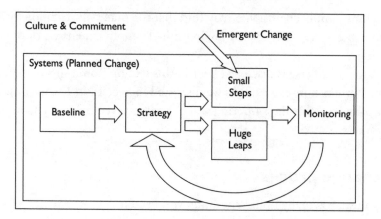

Figure 3.1 The components of our change management system

Creating a Culture for Change

Organizational culture

Nobody really likes change. More precisely, nobody really likes the thought of change, unless there is a clear benefit for them personally. Put lots of people together and this dislike increases exponentially. I call this 'institutional inertia', the force of will in any organization that pushes back against any change whether it is for the better or for the worse.

Your objective is to overcome this inertia and make each of your staff members a positive agent for change – part of the solution, not part of the problem.

There are two main issues here:

1   making a commitment (and being seen to 'walk the walk');
2   engaging your staff and making them part of the solution.

The good news is that employees like working for greener companies.[18] From the psychological high of being a force for good, through to the physiological benefits of some green business practices (more natural daylight, improved indoor air quality), there are numerous pluses for your employees. It should be relatively easy to persuade your staff to help you make the change.

Make sure that the tone of any campaign matches your company culture. For example, publisher Harper Collins decided that a fun, upbeat attitude was best for them (they call it 'stilettos, not sandals'),[19] whereas an engineering company may require a more data intensive approach.

Making a commitment

Commitment from the top

Too often I have seen embattled quality/health and safety/whatever managers being told to 'sort out this environmental business' and then being left to get on with it. Sometimes they succeed by bringing in some substantial quick wins and persuading the managing director to take the whole issue much more seriously.

Generally, though, to make any progress, the environmental function will require backing, both moral and financial, from the top management in the company – particularly if they want to get on to the 'huge leaps'. As with all change management, consistency of the message is essential, as is seeing those in responsible positions walking the walk.

If you are a manager you should consider making an obvious commitment such as using a bicycle or buying a hybrid car.

Financial commitment

While small steps will save you money at little or no cost, the huge leaps will require investment. While investments will be repaid in one way or another (even in the form of legal compliance), the risks they present must be understood.

One approach that has been successful is to provide a fighting fund which is topped up from a proportion of financial savings. In other words, if the fund invests in a new compressed air system leading to savings, then, say, 50 per cent of the savings every year go back into the fund. Woking Council in the UK have been operating such a fund for 13 years and have managed to save over £1m and cut carbon emissions from council buildings by 77.4 per cent.[20]

Environmental policy

An environmental policy is a written statement outlining an organization's mission in relation to managing the environmental impacts of its operations. It is usually seen in the foyers of their offices and on their websites. All forms of Environmental Management System (EMS) require an environmental policy as the bedrock of the system.

A policy is your public declaration of your commitment to improving your environmental performance, so it must be drafted carefully. There is no standard format for writing an environmental policy, but the style should reflect your organization's culture. When I write environmental policies for companies, I generally collect examples of policies written by other similar organizations and select the content, format and style most appropriate to the client.

There are a few basic tips to follow to ensure the policy is clearly written and concise:

- Keep the statement short – if it's longer than a sheet of A4, then it's probably too long.
- Make sure it is easy to read and understand.
- Be realistic, achievable and relevant to your organization's activities and practices.
- Demonstrate your commitment to making the policy work and get the statement signed, dated and endorsed by the managing director, Chief Executive or other senior manager.

As a general rule, the policy should contain:

- a commitment to continuous improvement (small steps);
- recognition of compliance with relevant environmental legislation as a minimum level of performance;
- a commitment to education and training of employees in environmental issues and the environmental effects of their activities;
- a commitment to the monitoring of progress.

Some people put in quite prescriptive commitments in their policies such as:

- use of timber from sustainable (managed) forests;
- phasing out of chlorofluorocarbons (CFCs) and ozone-depleting substances.

I only recommend this where the requirements are specific to the company's core business, such as a commitment to only using Forest Stewardship Council (FSC) approved wood if you make wooden products.

Envirowise[21] recommends the following list of statements as a starting point for a generic environmental policy:

- comply with the requirements of environmental legislation and approved codes of practice;

- assess the environmental impact of all historic, current and likely future operations;
- continuously seek to improve environmental performance;
- reduce pollution, emissions and waste;
- reduce the use of all raw materials, energy and supplies;
- raise awareness, encourage participation and train employees in environmental matters;
- expect similar environmental standards from all suppliers and contractors;
- assist customers to use products and services in an environmentally sensitive way;
- liaise with the local community;
- participate in discussions about environmental issues.

Overcoming internal resistance

If key individuals in your organization think that the environment is only for be-sandalled tree huggers, then don't panic, you just have to take another tack. Don't mention the environment. Ever. Instead you need to talk in purely business terms such as:

- 'Do you know that we are wasting £20,000 on energy every year?'
- 'Have you seen how much they're charging us for hazardous waste? Do you think it's time to phase out hazardous materials?'
- 'Our biggest client has just sent a supplier's questionnaire asking for our environmental policy.'
- 'The environmental regulators are here and they want to talk to you.'

You can then build a 'resource management system' rather than an environmental management system and use other such subterfuge to green the business without anyone knowing about it.

You will obviously still be hamstrung in terms of creating a genuine change culture and may be unable to communicate what you are doing, but you should be able to deliver most of what is in this book with the right amount of 'spin'.

Staff engagement

Why engage your staff?

When I walk around industrial sites, I often see water hoses left on, unused equipment left running and cool room doors left open. All of these have environmental and economic impacts and all are down to poor staff performance.

You can look at this from another angle as well. Many factories and offices have droves of workers toiling away at their little cog in the big machine that is your operation. Occasionally they get encouraged or chastised by someone in a suit. But these people probably know your operations better than you do, so ask them how things can be improved. The combined knowledge and experience of your staff is inevitably greater than yours. Many will walk past bad practice every day wondering 'Why does nobody fix that?'. You'll have a happier, more productive workforce and you may be surprised by the results.

Lastly, but most importantly, if you do want to make some of the radical changes proposed in this book, you will need to bring your staff with you if you want to do it effectively.

How to engage your staff

Every couple of weeks or so I get a call asking me whether I can run a lunchtime staff engagement session. And my answer is always 'Yes, but...'

The reason for that 'but' is that deciding to do staff engagement is a bit like realizing you are out of shape and joining a gym. You can't expect to get fit on the first session – in fact you are more likely to hate it and go back to your old habits. A training programme, self-discipline and changes to the rest of your lifestyle will be required to make the change properly.

Staff engagement is vital to greening your business, but there is no magic pill. Figure 3.2 shows that you need to have some form of intervention to shift people from their current behaviour and into the behaviour patterns you're after. But to keep them there you need reinforcement or they will quickly slip back into their old ways. It is the second of these principles that is most often overlooked, hence my 'but' when clients ask me to do a lunchtime seminar.

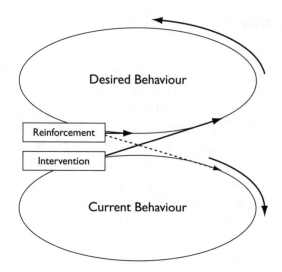

Figure 3.2 Behavioural change

Reinforcement

We'll look at reinforcement first as it is the key issue to sustaining the desired staff behaviour (although as we will see, good interventions make reinforcement easier). There are four types of reinforcement:

1   alignment of all systems to the goal: there is little point in trying to cut unnecessary car use if your allowances reward excessive mileage;
2   information: providing feedback on progress;
3   leadership: demonstrating personal commitment to the objectives and being intolerant of poor commitment from others. Leadership also means delegating responsibility and authority to the best effect;
4   self-reinforcement: when individuals or groups start to make the desired behaviour a habit.

Self-reinforcement is the ultimate goal of change management, but you will normally need the other pieces in place before you can achieve it.

Intervention

There are a number of options for intervention:

- proclamation from the top: this is the least effective method and it will take very strong leadership to succeed without the 'softer' forms of staff engagement;
- incentivization: providing rewards for good behaviour can have a big impact but beware of unintended consequences (see below);
- training and awareness: these can range from the dull and worthy through to the sublime. we'll discuss some ways below of how they can be made most effective;
- guerrilla methods: these are cunning ways of making people think about their behaviour without preaching;
- peer to peer: allowing your staff to spread the message through informal social networks in the workplace.

If you take a purely top-down approach to achieving reinforcement you will come up against resistance, cynicism and possibly outright rebellion. Here are some proven strategies for creating enthusiasm for the new regime among your staff:

- ownership of the solutions: if you engage staff in developing low carbon solutions for your organization, they will take pride in implementing them. problem solving can make staff engagement much more effective;
- delegation of responsibility: delegating decision making (and even some budget) to a staff committee;
- equity and fairness: if sacrifice is required, make sure that the management level takes at least their fair share of the pain;
- fun: make it 'more stilettos than sandals'. Play games, hold competitions or give out awards.

The better the intervention, the easier it is to achieve self-reinforcement. The following sections describe how to implement some of these intervention and reinforcement methods to best effect.

Training and awareness sessions

Done well, training and awareness sessions will help spell out why the green agenda is important to all staff and the business. Done badly and you may find increased cynicism. I always ensure that training sessions have a practical outcome by spending most of the session getting the participants to apply the lessons to their own organization or department. This not only makes the training more relevant, but can be a useful source of ideas, particularly for small steps. If these ideas are implemented then staff members will have pride in the results and are more likely to support than undermine them. This approach combines intervention and a strong element of self-reinforcement into one neat package.

Staff committees and champions

Taking this principle a step further, staff committees can be an extremely powerful tool for staff engagement and, indeed, implementing small steps. The committee must be tasked with identifying areas of concerns and developing solutions, and indeed engaging other staff members. Setting up such a committee will bring with it delegation of responsibility, gives the committee members ownership of the problems and solutions and encourages peer to peer communication. Committee membership should be chosen carefully to reflect all those who are required to make the change happen.

The Terra Infirma brainstorming tool was developed to aid problem and solution identification in group settings. It is described in Appendix 3. You may find that using an external facilitator to run each session can help prevent the committee turning into a general griping session or a workforce/management debate. Giving the committee a budget will give the committee status, esteem and a sense of purpose.

Appointing a 'green champion' in each department with the responsibility of communicating environmental messages is another form of peer to peer communication. Champions can of course constitute the committee membership, combining the two roles.

Action teams

In order to carry out more rigorous analysis such as creating a vision and the implementation of 'huge leaps', project teams will need to be created. While staff committees are permanent 'think tanks', action teams are time-limited 'task and finish' groups of people, who complete their task and disband. More details are given in Chapter 5, but the principle is the same as a committee, ownership of the problems and their solutions is given to staff members.

Incentives

Providing incentives for any form of work performance is fraught with the danger of unintended consequences and perceived unfairness. For example if you reward one member of staff for a waste-saving idea, chances are that at least three others will grumble that they had been saying that for years but no-one had listened. If you reward staff for not commuting by car, you may suffer from a backlash from people who genuinely need a car to care for a relative. However, a number of simple incentive systems have been used successfully:

- a suggestion scheme with a monthly or annual prize for the best idea put forward;
- docking the budgets of any department who do not act in an eco-friendly way. This is obviously dangerous and the criteria have to be clearly defined;
- providing a small fund (say £100 a year per employee) for any member of staff to implement a green idea.

On the other hand, there is quite a strong body of opinion that suggests you are better off engaging staff in business improvement properly than providing financial incentives. Listening to what they think, challenging them to come up with solutions and saying 'thanks' may have a more positive effect than doling out cash.

Guerrilla methods

Guerrilla methods are designed to disrupt the habits of staff members by confronting them with an unexpected situation. For example some companies started their energy efficiency intervention by putting a chocolate on the keyboard of everyone who switched their computer off at night with no expla-nation. The resulting water cooler debates – 'what was that all about?' – made everyone stop and think about the message the chocolates conveyed.

This type of guerrilla method is best designed and implemented by staff committees and/or champions as a managerial intervention of this sort can lead to a perceived naffness. Therefore they can be a form of peer to peer communication as well – peers will have a better feel for what will work in the workplace culture.

Sustainability expert John Ehrenfeld proposes that forcing people to make choices between more and less sustainable options engages them directly with the consequences of their actions.[22] He illustrates this with the example of the dual flush toilet – instead of a single button there are two: one provides a high volume flush, the other a low volume flush. Every time someone uses the toilet they have to decide 'do I use lots of water or a small amount of water?' which prompts the question 'why is this important?' This principle can be extended to all sorts of workplace examples, for example recycling bins, reusable stationery or fleet vehicles.

Feedback

An important plank of reinforcement is to provide feedback on environmental issues to your staff. For example continuous displays of energy consumption on public display screens, updates on the company intranet or, more simply, graphs of monthly performance in places where people tend to linger, for example by coffee machines, water coolers, staff rooms or the mail room. Emphasize the cost of these issues to the business so you win over the cynical as well as the open minded.

Top ten tips for culture change

- Make a commitment through an environmental policy.
- Keep the policy to one page of A4.
- Go out of your way to 'walk the walk', even when the going gets tough.
- Engage your staff and make them part of the solution.
- Make an appropriate financial commitment.
- Set up staff committees to develop 'small steps'.
- Set up action teams for 'huge leaps'.
- Implement simple incentive schemes, but with great care.
- Provide feedback to all staff.
- Match your tone to the company culture.

Environmental Management Systems

Purpose of an EMS

An environmental management system (EMS) is a framework for measuring environmental impacts, setting objectives, developing and implementing action plans and monitoring the result. There are a number of formal EMS standards such as ISO 14001 and the Environmental Management and Audit System (EMAS). While there is no necessity to follow such a standard, it makes sense to follow a recognized approach in case you decide to later. The resulting certificate is a powerful statement to your stakeholders both inside and outside the organization.

Implementing an EMS is not for the faint-hearted and it is just an enabling mechanism rather than an end in itself. A cynic once told me 'an EMS allows you to destroy the environment in a well documented manner'. There is some truth in this – while EMS standards require continual improvement (small steps), none requires compliance with any absolute limit stricter than the law of the land and none expects you to make major changes to your product, process or facilities.

This section lays out the basic principles of an EMS and gives some tips on how to approach developing and maintaining one. However a step-by-step guide would take a book in itself and there are plenty available (see Appendix 1). Note that most organizations employ an external consultancy firm to get an EMS up and running. I generally advise my clients to do the same (and it is not a service I offer!).

EMS standards

The most popular type of EMS for business is ISO 14001 which is very similar in structure to the ISO 9000 Quality standards and ISO 18000 Health & Safety standard.

EMAS is more prescriptive and tends to be used by public sector organizations. The scheme was launched in April 1995 and revised in 2001 to incorporate ISO

14001 as its environmental management system component. EMAS goes beyond ISO 14001 in a number of ways. It requires organizations to:

- undertake an initial environmental review;
- actively involve employees in implementing EMAS;
- make relevant information available to the public and other parties.

I recommend that you choose ISO 14001 over EMAS as it is more widely recognized and can be integrated with its Quality Assurance and Health & Safety equivalents. Given the time and effort required to set up an EMS, smaller organizations can follow an incrementally implemented standard BS 8555. This provides a series of certification steps from commitment through to ISO 14001, which is attained at the end of the process.

How EMSs work

The main clauses of ISO 14001

ISO 14001 has the following main clauses:

- policy: this forms the bedrock of the system;
- planning: identify legal requirements and major environmental impacts, set objectives and targets;
- implementation and operation: documentation of roles and responsibilities, procedures for operations, emergency procedures, document control and training/awareness;
- checking and corrective action: procedures for monitoring and measuring impacts, correcting non-conformances and auditing the system;
- management review: reviews the effectiveness of the EMS in the face of changing internal and external factors. Identifies changes required to maintain that effectiveness.

Policy underpins the whole system and the other clauses are followed in a loop – following the 'Deming Cycle' of 'Plan, Do, Check, Act' (see Figure 3.3). At each stage of the loop, the procedures that you put in place to operate the system must

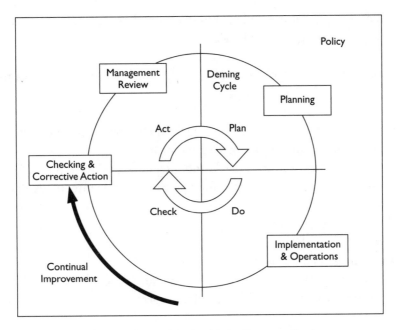

Figure 3.3 ISO14001 and the Deming Cycle

be documented. The ISO 9001 Quality Assurance System and ISO 18000 Health & Safety standards are also based on the Deming Cycle, so the three can easily be combined.

Compliance with legislation

It is a requirement of ISO 14001 to maintain a register of legislation which applies to the operations within the EMS. I recommend you use a simple table or spreadsheet to record important information about legal requirements, for example:

- the name of the regulation, legislation or code of practice and date of effect;
- how it applies to your organization, process or activity;
- the name and phone number of the person responsible for compliance;

- references to procedures and operations manuals to manage and control operations relating to compliance.

Once you have a table, you have to identify which legislation applies to your operations, such as (in the UK):

- waste duty of care: you are responsible for the proper disposal of your waste (every business comes under this legislation);
- integrated pollution control (IPC) and integrated pollution prevention and control (IPPC) legislation: these apply to certain environmentally damaging processes;
- effluent discharge consents;
- water abstraction licence(s);
- waste management licence(s);
- other waste regulations, e.g. packaging regulations, Waste Electrical and Electronic Equipment (WEEE) regulations, etc.

If you are concerned about other legislation that might apply to your operations, then contact the Environment Agency (for England and Wales) or your national equivalent. The NetRegs website (www.netregs.gov.uk) is a useful source of information on UK legislation. In other countries you should contact your national environmental regulator.

Pollution prevention

It may appear obvious, but all EMSs require a commitment to prevent pollution. This means that any company that is found to be blatantly polluting the environment (e.g. through leaks) will not achieve their ISO 14001 certification.

Continual improvement

ISO 14001 requires continuous improvement of environmental performance year on year. Auditors will expect to see evidence of how performance has improved. This is where many companies trip up as it becomes more difficult year on year to show an incremental improvement. Eventually you may be forced into taking a 'huge leap' in order to keep moving forward.

Top ten tips for EMS

- Get proper commitment from the top.
- Make sure everyone understands the commitment to continual improvement.
- Make sure the system is properly resourced.
- If you employ consultants, make sure they deliver an elegant, easy-to-use system.
- Use an EMS as a framework for small steps and to monitor the results of huge leaps.
- Get the system running smoothly before going for certification.
- Engage as many staff as possible in the process.
- If you do not intend to go for certification, it is a good idea to base your EMS on ISO 14001 so you can change your mind at a later date.
- If resources are limited, consider BS 8555 so you can phase in an EMS over a period of time.
- Integrate the process into quality and health and safety management systems where possible to save resources.

Measuring Performance

Measuring your impact

There is an old managerial maxim:

> If you can't measure it, you can't manage it.

Environmental management is no different. You will need to measure a baseline to determine your starting point and then monitor progress against that baseline.

There are many, many ways of measuring your environmental impact, but they fall into three types:

1 Measuring a wide range of Key Performance Indicators (KPIs).
2 Proxy indicators: using a smaller number of broad brush indicators to represent wider environmental performance (e.g. carbon footprint).
3 Aggregated indicators: these attempt to add the apples and oranges of different environmental parameters into a single score.

But you must not focus exclusively on numbers. There are a number of qualitative, less tangible aspects to your environmental performance that you will need to factor in as well. Some examples are:

● public perception of your business;
● aesthetic qualities of your facilities;
● staff attitudes.

Why establish a baseline?

Measuring and understanding your baseline is the essential first step in greening an existing business. The information will:

- give you an understanding of what the big issues are;
- inform the development of your environmental vision and policy;
- help you identify some early quick wins and create momentum.

Key performance indicators

This is the easiest and the most robust way of determining impacts, but it is difficult to trade between different parameters, e.g. how do you compare water pollution with carbon emissions? Potential indicators include:

- solid waste arisings either in terms of volume or mass;
- hazardous solid/liquid waste arisings – volume;
- the Biological/Chemical Oxygen Demand (BOD/COD) of effluent;
- volume of effluent;
- data from monitoring of stack emissions, for example particulates;
- consumption of gas, oil and electricity;
- fleet mileage;
- consumption of water.

Carbon footprinting

What is a carbon footprint?

A carbon footprint is the total amount of greenhouse gas, expressed in terms of equivalent amounts of carbon dioxide, for which an individual, organization, product or event is responsible.

When it comes to carbon footprints, the 'Greenhouse Gas Protocol' is regarded as the bible.[23] The six greenhouse gases as laid down in the protocol are:

1 Carbon dioxide (CO_2);
2 Methane (CH_4);
3 Nitrous oxide (N_2O);
4 Hydrofluorocarbons (HFCs);
5 Perfluorocarbons (PFCs);
6 Sulphur hexafluoride (SF_6).

The Greenhouse Gas Protocol specifies four types of emissions that should be included:

Scope 1. Direct emissions: these include carbon dioxide emissions from burning fossil fuels, powering vehicles or other equipment. Other emissions may come from chemical reactions, fugitive emissions (leaks) or the decomposition of organic materials (e.g. in composting);

Scope 2. Indirect emissions from use of electricity: virtually every person or organization uses electricity to power equipment, heating and lighting. If this electricity comes from the mains then the amount of carbon dioxide emitted in the power stations to produce that electricity must be factored in to the footprint;

Scope 3. Indirect emissions from products and services: every organization that supplies the organization under consideration will have its own carbon footprint made up of direct emissions, indirect emissions from electricity and indirect emissions from its own suppliers.

In addition, some organizations include emissions outside those stipulated by the Protocol;

Scope 4. Emissions from the use of the products and services you provide.

Choosing the scope of your footprint

Despite the fact that many businesses (including some major supermarket chains) stop at Scope 2, I believe that the absolute minimum that a business should include is Scope 3. The whole idea of the 'footprint' concept is to convey

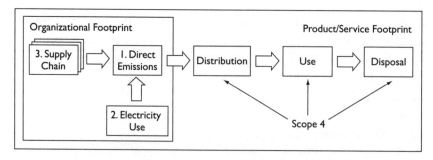

Figure 3.4 Different scopes of carbon footprints

the entire impact of the organization, not just selected parts of it. In addition Scope 3 tends to dominate the footprint for many organizations, for example in the UK's National Health Service, Scope 3 represents 60 per cent of its footprint.[24] For those who want to be a truly green business then the whole cradle to grave footprint should be taken, in other words, Scopes 1–4.

The inclusion of indirect emissions from the entire supply chain raises one very difficult question – where do you stop? If you start to list the number of potential sources of greenhouse gases among your suppliers, their suppliers etc, you will soon realize that this is a very data intensive exercise. I recommend the following shortcuts to prevent the exercise becoming unmanageable:

● 80/20 thinking: if your company consumes a large amount of energy intensive material (e.g. aluminium) and a tiny amount of low energy services (e.g. contractors who carry out an annual site audit), then it is reasonable to count the production of aluminium in and exclude the contractors

● use of published data: if your suppliers already publish their carbon footprint then it is reasonable to use a pro rata amount of this. If you can find data from a study on a similar organization, you can use that as long as you document the source and the justification for using it.

Making assumptions

When you start calculating a carbon footprint, you will find that you need to make assumptions: for example the expected lifespan of your product, how users will use or abuse your product or service, what proportion of each supplier's footprint relates to the product or service they sell to you, etc. After the scope, these assumptions have the next biggest effect on your results.

Life cycle assumptions are particularly difficult to make. Products ranging from mobile phones to ships become economically obsolete (they go out of fashion or become too expensive to maintain) long before they become physically obsolete (i.e. they break). Other products have almost infinite lives, for example, almost every Rolls Royce ever built still exists.

Some published data is also controversial, for example the standard figure for the carbon intensity of electricity in the UK has been 0.43kg CO_2 per unit (kWh). However the UK government released figures in 2007 that suggested the real figure was closer to 0.53 kg CO_2 per unit.[25] Some commentators argue that this does not take into account transmission losses, and the real figure is closer to 1 kg CO_2 per unit.[26]

The golden rules of making assumptions are:

- be consistent: any assumption should be applied to all relevant elements of the footprint, not just where it suits best;
- be transparent: the source or logic behind each assumption should be documented;
- be conservative: when in doubt you should choose the assumption that will make your footprint larger rather than smaller.

The effect of each assumption can be tested using sensitivity analysis. The data arising from the assumption is changed by a small amount and its influence on the results measured. Assumptions with a significant effect on the results can then be analysed further to ensure they are robust.

Ecological footprinting

Ecological footprinting expresses the environmental impact of your operations as the theoretical area of the Earth's surface required to support them. It is usually composed of the following:

- the actual land taken up by buildings and physical infrastructure such as roads;
- the actual land required to produce food, fibre and forestry products;
- the theoretical amount of forested land required to recycle all our carbon dioxide emissions back into oxygen.

For many businesses, land use is not a major environmental issue compared to their other impacts. If you make significant use of food, fibre and forestry products in your business (e.g. if you are a supermarket or in the clothing industry), then the ecological footprint may be a more comprehensive indicator than the carbon footprint, otherwise stick with the latter.

Aggregated indicators

These indicators (e.g. Eco-indicator 95)[27] attempt to combine a wide range of environmental impacts (e.g. climate change, acid rain, eco-toxic effects) into a single score using subjective weighting. They were in fashion in the 1990s, but have fallen out of favour as they lack transparency and are highly dependent on the weights given to the different effects. I don't recommend them as a rule.

Conclusion

Measuring your environmental performance and that of your products is essential so you can manage it and communicate it to your stakeholders. If you are in the food, fibre or forestry industry, start with the ecological footprint as a measure, otherwise use the carbon footprint. Augment the footprint with direct measurements (e.g. waste sent to landfill, water consumption) to focus action.

Lastly, there is an old farmers' saying that is the flip side to 'if you can't measure it, you can't manage it' and it goes:

No-one ever fattened a pig by weighing it.

In other words, don't get fooled into thinking that measurement alone will green your business. You need to act as well.

Creating a Strategy

The tyranny of the present

In Chapter 2 we saw how, despite the need for huge leaps to hit the requirements for sustainability, most companies merely deliver incremental improvements at best. This is due to the forecasting approach most people take in planning – working out which way the trends are going and trying to 'bend the trend' (see Figure 3.5). So how do we identify the huge leaps and avoid potential cul-de-sacs along the way?

One good way to escape 'the tyranny of the present' is to start with your ultimate goal and work backwards to today – a method known as *backcasting*. Backcasting attempts to ensure that barriers and current trends should only influence the pace and initial scale of the transition, not its direction.

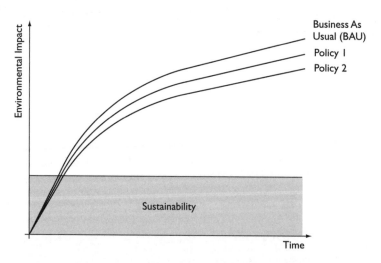

Figure 3.5 Incremental policies resulting from forecasting

Backcasting: Starting at the end

Backcasting sets up desirable future scenarios and then attempts to map policy paths back to the current situation (see Figure 3.6). This is a 'normative' approach – it focuses on defining desirable outcomes and making them 'the norm', rather than struggling with current trends.[28] The term 'backcasting' is generally credited to John Robinson[29] who formalized the methodology behind the 'soft energy paths' work of US energy guru Amory Lovins in the 1970s.

The benefits of backcasting are that it is:

- strategic: policies are developed with a long term view;
- holistic: policies are developed in compatible packages rather than as individual initiatives;
- proactive: the focus is on a desirable outcome rather than trying to buck trends;
- participative: backcasting is highly suitable for engaging a range of staff and possibly other stakeholders in the strategy process;
- creative: by forgetting current trends, the scope for innovative, 'out of the box' thinking is maximized.

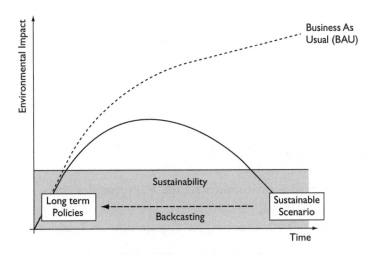

Figure 3.6 Backcasting[30]

The following steps are involved in backcasting:

- define a vision of a sustainable future (examples: Solar, Cyclic, Safe; or factor 10);
- develop scenarios which describe how that vision could be met;
- determine the organization's current position in relation to that idealized future;
- develop strategic paths to meet that future, i.e. define the steps required on the staircase model, avoiding cul-de-sacs (see Secret No 3);
- identify policies, projects and programmes to start the company along the strategic path from the current position.

The backcasting approach lends itself to a collaborative, brainstorming approach. The development of scenarios, strategic paths and projects is typically done in multi-disciplinary workshops. It is imperative to make sure that participants really understand the difference between backcasting and forecasting to ensure the sessions do not get stuck in the present.

Using backcasting for green business strategy

Strategy development team

To use backcasting you will need to put together a strategy development team. For example, you may want to include:

- product/service designers;
- production team/operations staff;
- environmental staff;
- business development staff;
- sales and marketing staff;
- external experts (e.g. environmental experts, process designers, lean manufacturing experts);
- external stakeholders (customers, pressure groups, local residents);

- a facilitator: an external facilitator is more likely to be seen as an honest broker and may help avoid the process getting bogged down in company politics.

Workshops

You will need a series of workshops for the strategy development team supported by background research to inform decisions. A typical three-workshop process is:

Workshop 1: Analyse your baseline and develop the endpoint. Scope out candidate scenarios.
– Background research: analyse the implications of the candidate scenarios, identify any showstoppers

Workshop 2: Fine tune and agree scenarios. Develop lists of candidate solutions (using Chapters 4 and 5 of this book) to deliver those scenarios.
– Background research: evaluate the candidate solutions against business criteria including cost benefit analysis and risk

Workshop 3: Fine tune and agree solutions.
– Completion: turn the outputs of Workshop 3 into an action plan, get management approval and launch the necessary implementation action teams.

You can use the brainstorming checklists in the Appendix 2 to help the teams develop the policies.

Scenarios

Once you have an endpoint you need to develop scenarios which meet the endpoint. Your scenarios will be highly dependent on your business sector, but typical endpoint scenarios include:

- techno-fix: you maintain the same way of doing business, but technology delivers all the changes required (e.g. using efficient equipment, renewable energy, etc);
- changed business model: the scenario involves changing the service provided to the client/customer, e.g. moving from selling cars to selling travel services;

- distributed business: moving from a centralized system to one distributed across its geographical area and delivering more localized services.

By using different scenarios and carrying out a risk analysis, you can use the backcasting method to choose the 'best' strategy to follow.

External Communication

Spreading the word

Being a green business may save you money and give you and your staff a warm glow, but if you do not communicate what you are doing outside the business you may be missing out. There are many forms of external communication:

- general environmental performance: this is to give a 'warm feeling' to all interested parties – employees, potential employees, regulators, clients/customers, investors, local communities, etc;
- stakeholder engagement: a two-way communication on a particular issue (for example planning a new facility);
- targeted marketing of your products and/or services as 'green'.

This is a dangerous area and many large businesses have come a cropper, including Monsanto, Shell and Ryanair as we shall see. There's nothing that the press and public like more than seeing pride before a fall.

The hyenas will circle

There are many people out there who love to see 'green' businesses exposed as 'un-green'. They include:

- fundamentalist greens who believe that business is intrinsically 'bad' environmentally and see any attempt to build a green business as 'greenwash';
- the sensationalist press who know that a story entitled, say, 'organic food exposed!' will sell newspapers and magazines;
- reactionary smart-alecs who just want to be cleverer than everyone else;
- unscrupulous business rivals who see green companies starting to eat into their market share and want to undermine them. Note that in extreme cases, front organizations are used to do the dirty work.

In my experience, none of these types is particularly bothered about the accuracy of their claims. I recommend you see them as a spur to make sure that your green offering is as robust as possible and rebut any unfounded allegations in a sober manner, using third-party assessments/accreditations wherever possible.

Understanding your audiences

Types of belief

Attitudes towards the environment and sustainable development vary across a wide spectrum. Social scientists use a fourfold typology to describe beliefs about society and nature, each belief being defined by the degree of equality and individualism. Figure 3.7 illustrates this with a ball representing the state of the environment. If the ball is moved a little bit (an environmental impact), then it will either stay where it is (another stable state), return to its original position, or drop off the model (ecological disaster).

The four attitudes are:

1   Individualist: the environment is benign, robust and there to be exploited. Use as much of it as you can. This is the traditional industrial approach and that of 'climate change deniers';

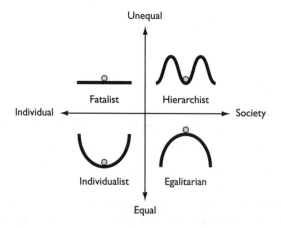

Figure 3.7 Cultural theory: Fourfold typology[31]

2 Hierarchist: the environment is there to be exploited but has to be protected to remain within limits. Typical approach of governments and public sector bodies;
3 Egalitarian: the environment is fragile and requires protection. Environmental damage must be minimized at all costs. Typical approach of environmental pressure groups;
4 Fatalist: the environment shifts from one state to another, but none is any better or worse than any other. Fatalists feel they have no power over their lives.

Table 3.1 describes in more detail the attitudes of the first three of these attitudes (the fatalist doesn't care so isn't included).

Sustainability lies somewhere between the hierarchist (present = future) and egalitarian (the risk averse nature of the Precautionary Principle) categories. You can still appeal to the individualist using the 'What's In It For Me?' principle.

Risk perception

Risk is a particularly problematic area when it comes to communication. Engineers traditionally calculate risk as:

Risk = probability of an impact happening × severity of that impact

This assumes that lots of small risks are perceived as the same as one big risk. However, the general public and the press see low probability/high impact risks

Table 3.1 *Summary of cultural attitudes*

	Egalitarian	Individualist	Hierarchist
Decision criteria	Argument	Experience	Evidence
Management style	Preventive	Adaptive	Controlling
Distribution of resources	Parity	Priority	Proportionality
Perception of time	Present < future	Present > future	Present = future
View of resources	Depleting	Abundant	Scarce
Attitude towards risk	Risk averse	Risk seeking	Risk accepting

(e.g. a plane crash) while ignoring high probability/low impact risks (car crashes). The difference between these two views is down to risk perception.

The following factors are known to affect people's perception of risk (described relative to a 'scientific' judgement of risk):[32]

- familiarity: people tend to underestimate familiar risks and overestimate unfamiliar ones;
- control: people tend to underestimate risks over which they have control;
- proximity in space: people overestimate risks close to them leading to the Not In My Back Yard (NIMBY) syndrome;
- proximity in time: people tend to ignore delayed consequences of risks;
- the dread factor: people tend to exaggerate risks from phenomena they do not understand;
- the scale factor: the general public and the media tend to be more concerned with one large-scale consequence than many smaller consequences with the same overall magnitude.

Looking back at cultural theory, a hierarchist view of risk would be given by the 'engineering' view of risk. Uncertainty in the variables would be taken into consideration. Much risk assessment is carried out in this way, for example in the offshore industry.

The egalitarian view includes the perception of risks by the general public and non-governmental organizations (NGOs). The descriptions of risk perception factors above were quoted from a government (and most likely hierarchist) document which assumes that the 'scientific' estimation of risks is the 'correct' one. This should be borne in mind when interpreting the words 'overestimate' and 'underestimate' in their descriptions. However, the cultural theory approach works on the basis that all cultural views are equally valid. The human perception of risk has evolved over millions of years and the instinctive reaction to risk should not be ignored. The Precautionary Principle also promotes this point of view.

You must bear in mind all these attitudes to the environment and risk when communicating with the public and other stakeholders. For example, Monsanto spent millions on public engagement for genetically modified (GM) crops in the 1990s. They presented their products as potential solutions to famines and world poverty. Risks were presented in a 'hierarchist' manner, quoting research results. However the plan did not succeed as the public's *perception* of the risks from 'frankenstein foods', as they were dubbed by pressure groups, outweighed the benefits which Monsanto presented. Monsanto eventually pulled out of Europe altogether in 2003.[33]

Communicating performance

The purpose of communicating environmental performance is to demonstrate that you are serious about improving your environmental performance. The audiences for the communication include employees, potential employees, regulators, customers, potential customers, investors and local communities.

Methods of communicating

Some examples of methods of communicating environmental performance are:

- annual Corporate Social Responsibility (CSR), environmental or sustainability reports;
- on-line: websites, blogs, viral marketing methods;
- internal communication channels: intranets, e-mails, company circulars, on-site display boards and screens;
- keynote speeches at conferences (or indeed sponsoring/hosting conferences);
- traditional media: press releases, press conferences, advertising on TV, radio and hoardings;
- information on packaging and product documentation;
- information on 'transactional collateral', e.g. tickets, bills, invoices and receipts.

Choice of language

It is a truism that different words mean different things to different people. Meanings and understanding evolve constantly. For example, the term carbon footprint is now constantly used casually in the media, but five years ago it would have been met with a wall of incomprehension.

Choose your words carefully to resonate with all levels of understanding and the different cultural attitudes to the environment.

Communicating your performance: Top tips

- Don't overstate your case or you will play into the hands of the hyenas.
- Avoid nonsensical phrases like 'help us save the environment'. You're not that powerful.
- Eco-clichés turn people off. Personally I never want to see a picture of hands cupping a sapling ever again.
- Acknowledge your shortfalls. There's nothing worse than a self-congratulatory report on a year which has included a well-publicized pollution incident.
- Get third-party accreditation for your claims wherever possible.

Stakeholder engagement

Proactive communication is a key part of successful environmental management. A stakeholder is any person or group of persons with an interest in your business. Stakeholders can be divided into the following categories:

- Strategic stakeholders can affect the performance of the company, for example governments, regulatory bodies, finance companies, etc.
- Moral stakeholders are those affected by the company's activities. A balance of interests is required. Examples include local populations, environmental pressure groups, etc.

The expensive failure of many recent public relations blitzes, such as the Monsanto's failure described above, has led to many companies adopting a more proactive stakeholder management policy. This involves understanding the needs, motivations and fears of each stakeholder rather than trying to simply bulldoze them into submission.

Engendering trust

Trust is key to good stakeholder engagement. Factors affecting trust include:

- perceived competence, e.g. degree of technical expertise;
- objectivity: lack of bias in information;
- fairness;

- consistency: don't get cold feet if the decisions get tough;
- faith: goodwill, or you do what you say you will do.

One trap that many fall into when working with stakeholders is to raise expectations too high. If stakeholders start to believe that they have the ultimate say, they will get very angry if and when they are told they can't have what they want. Tell them clearly: 'We are listening to you, but at the end of the day we have to make the decisions, and sometimes we will disagree.'

Different levels of engagement

Figure 3.8 shows Arnstein's Ladder of Public Participation. While this is a model for public governance, it provides a useful structure to consider at what level you want to engage your stakeholders. The levels are:

- manipulation: the stakeholder is 'spun' a particular line, with selective information;
- information provision: objective information is provided to stakeholders so they can see the 'true' picture;
- consultation: stakeholders are asked for their views on a proposed solution. These are considered during the decision making process;

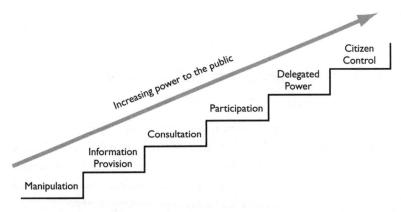

Figure 3.8 Arnstein's Ladder of Public Participation

- participation: stakeholders are given an opportunity to take part in the development of solutions and their views are considered during decision making;
- delegated power: stakeholders are given decision making powers over a limited number of issues;
- citizen control: stakeholders do all the decision making.

The appropriate level of engagement can be chosen for each stakeholder depending on the circumstances. For example:

- consumers may be provided with information on the product or service to help them make a choice;
- local residents may be consulted on a proposed new building;
- you may bring a pressure group in to participate in a joint project, for example Coca-Cola and World Wide Fund for Nature (WWF's) collaboration on water management in developing countries[34] which has turned a potential public relations disaster into a good news story;
- a conservation group may be given delegated power to manage an area on site for wildlife.

Smaller businesses will find it difficult to do more than provide information, but larger organizations should consider the full range of options. It is essential that the stakeholders know which level they are being engaged at and understand the limits of the influence they will have.

Marketing green products and services

The green graveyard

Unfortunately too many well-meaning products and services end up in what US green marketing guru Jacquelyn Ottman calls the 'Green Graveyard', making the fatal assumption that green credentials can overcome mediocre performance, poor design and, frankly, soppy branding. These products have fallen foul of the caveat in Secret No 1: 'Don't forget you are still running a business'.

Successful green products look good, perform well and are branded to make clear the benefits of the product to the user rather than the planet. To take an everyday example, the highly energy-efficient compact fluorescent light (CFL) bulb initially flopped. Its first major manufacturer, Phillips, packaged it as the 'Earth Light' with its box decorated with mountains and trees. Consumers did not buy it. A quick redesign of product and branding produced the 'Marathon', with its card festooned with claims of financial savings through long life and lower energy bills. It flew off the shelves and is fast becoming the standard type of bulb in many people's eyes.

The development of green markets

The problem facing the marketing of green products and services is their past (see Table 3.2). People still associate 'green' with undrinkable fair trade coffee from the 1980s and washing powders that just didn't work. These products and services were developed by well-meaning activists who had no qualms in eschewing a modern consumerist lifestyle for their belief in a low impact society.

Most green products are currently in a niche market, developed and marketed by entrepreneurs who believe in the environmental and business imperatives. Only a few products, such as the energy efficient white goods discussed above, organic baby food or The Body Shop's toiletries, have broken through into the mass market. The perception of many consumers that 'green' means 'shoddy' creates a huge hurdle for the entrepreneurs who want to sell to the mass market.

Table 3.2 *Green market development*[35]

Stage	Informal sector	Green niche		Mass market
Business actors	Voluntary activists	Green entrepreneurs		Professional manager
Customer attitudes	Customers will gladly sacrifice quality and price for eco-credentials	Customers will sacrifice some quality and price for eco-credentials	*Barrier*	Customers want quality and price first and see eco-credentials as a bonus

If you want to sell to a mass market, then you must market on traditional strengths: quality, price (high or low) or image. Use the environmental benefit of your product as a bonus, not the unique selling point.

On the other hand, if you *do* want to market your product to the green niche, then the green credentials should be put to the fore. I have been told by an ex-employee that one organic supermarket (now defunct) even used to unpack their flapjacks from their plastic containers and re-wrap them in cling film to make them look more 'homemade' and 'organic'. While I don't endorse such wasteful practices, it does demonstrate how you have to understand what your market wants.

The sizes of different markets

Green markets are constantly shifting and are highly dependent on the types of product and the marketing of those products. For example, The Body Shop built a strong market for green cosmetics, and the energy labelling of white goods has transformed that market (see below).

Recent green market surveys suggest that, as a rule of thumb:

- one-third of consumers see 'green' as good;
- one-third will follow the crowd, reluctantly or cautiously towards greener purchases;
- one-third are anti-green and/or completely oblivious to the green message.

Eco-labelling

Third-party accreditation is always a good back-up for your green claims. Eco-labels for products can have remarkable effects. The European Union's energy labels for white goods boosted the market share of A-rated products in the UK from 0 per cent in 1996/1997 to almost 80 per cent in 2005/2006.[36] This demonstrates the simple power of a good labelling system – who wants to have a 'D' rated product?

The A–G energy label is now being applied to a wide range of other products including windows, houses and even aircraft.

Other well-accepted eco-labels include:

- US energy star label: awarded to the most efficient models of electrical goods;

- European Union eco-label 'flower' covers a wide range of products and services including cleaning products, appliances, paper products, home furnishings, paints and garden (compost), clothing, tourism, lubricants (see Figure 3.9).
- Forest Stewardship Council (FSC): this shows that wood and wood products (including paper pulp) come from a sustainable source.
- Marine Stewardship Council (MSC): the equivalent of the FSC for marine products.
- Soil Association: there are a number of organic food accreditations, but in the UK at least, the Soil Association's label is the most respected.
- Green Globe 21: tourism destinations.

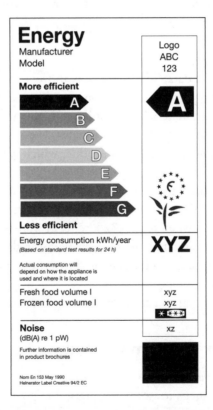

Figure 3.9 European Union energy label

There is a raft of more obscure equivalents, but I recommend sticking to the well-known labels.

Greenwashing

Don't make false or misleading claims for your product. For example it is very easy to manipulate life cycle environmental data by making unfair assumptions that count against competitors' products. This is known as WYGIWYN or 'What You Get Is What You Need'. In one infamous case, a marketing company 'proved' that a Hybrid Toyota Prius had a bigger carbon footprint per mile over its lifecycle than a General Motors Hummer.[37] It did this by assuming that Hummer drivers drove three times as much over the vehicle's life cycle. This exaggerated the higher energy required due to the manufacture of the Prius' battery by a factor of six.

What not to do:

- lie: don't be tempted;
- manipulate life cycle data: WYGIWYN as above;
- carry out selective reporting: OK, so your new product may be made from 100 per cent recycled material, but if it is also highly toxic, it would be a bit naughty to suggest it is 'green';
- be irrelevant: stating CFC-free on a product which is never likely to contain CFCs;
- overstate the case: Shell recently got in trouble with the UK Advertising Standards Agency (ASA) for implying that all of their CO_2 emissions were used to grow flowers when only 0.325 per cent were used in this way;[38]
- understate embarrassing information: Ryanair was also criticized by the ASA, but in their case it was for playing down the carbon footprint of the aviation industry;[39]
- be vague: simply saying you are green is not good enough. Prove it!

Top ten tips for green marketing

- Don't forget the hyenas; they will jump on any fault.
- For consumer products, resist the temptation to go overboard on the 'green look'.

- For business services and products, focus on business benefits such as reduced costs.
- Design your product and/or service so it/they can compete on performance and/or price.
- Market the product in an assured manner – if you are wishy-washy then that will reflect on your product.
- If you are targeting a green niche then do play the green card more strongly.
- Use eco-labels or other recognized accreditation wherever possible.
- Avoid spurious claims or overstating your case.
- Avoid vagueness.
- Publish data to back up your claims, for example on your website.

Chapter 4

Small Steps

Doing Things Right

Reality check

In this section you will learn techniques for improving your environmental performance without radically altering the way you do business. They are:

- pollution incident prevention;
- waste minimization and recycling;
- energy efficiency;
- water conservation;
- green procurement;
- green transport planning;
- carbon offsetting.

The environmental benefits of these techniques are incremental. Using them will make you a green*er* business, but not necessarily a *green* business – this will require the huge leaps in Chapter 5. Frankly, this is the stuff you should be doing anyway as most of these have significant economic benefits. Unfortunately my experience is that many businesses overlook these easy opportunities which will cut costs, reduce risks and get a little bit greener.

Barriers

There should be few obstacles to the small steps. Even if you don't have commitment from your management, they are typically low- or no-cost measures that will cut your operating costs, so should be easy to sell internally. However barriers include:

- Control over your premises: if you rent your premises, you may not be able to control heating, air conditioning and the disposal of waste. Your landlord may benefit more than you from environmental improvements, so you may have to negotiate with them to come up with a win-win agreement.

- Lack of staff buy-in: this can stymie your chances of sustaining change. This is why the staff engagement measures discussed in Chapter 3 are so important.
- Over-familiarity with your site(s) and operations. You may be walking past cost saving opportunities every day and never see them.

Implementation

This section contains excellent issues for a staff committee to take on. The checklists of the small steps and the lists of top tips in Appendix 2 can be used by the committee to stimulate thinking.

The other recommendations in Chapter 3 such as suggestion schemes and training may also produce easy to implement ideas. However you may want to complement your staff with the 'fresh pair of eyes' of an external expert. Such experts can also bring in ideas from other industries that you may not be aware of.

Pollution Incident Prevention

The cost of accidents

Pollution incidents cost a lot of money. When BP polluted groundwater in Leagrave, UK, the fine may have been a measly £8000, but the remediation cost £320,000.[40] The EasyJet entrepreneur Stelios Haji-Ioannou makes safety a number one priority. Asked why he spends so much on new jets and maintenance on his budget airline, he referred to the loss of one of his ferries when he worked for his father's shipping companies. 'If you think safety is expensive, you should try having an accident' he concluded.

As well as the economic cost, pollution incidents make very poor publicity, particularly in relation to local communities. Many companies talk about their 'licence to operate' coming from their closest neighbours; an accident is the quickest way to get that licence revoked. It is wise to remember the public's perception of risk, in particular the fact that one large incident is regarded as much worse than many small ones.

Note: If your business is mainly office based and/or does not involve storage of significant amounts of hazardous substances (such as oils or chemicals), you can probably skip this section.

Types of incident

For there to be an environmental impact, there has to be a source, pathway and a receptor (see Chapter 1). The pathway tends to be either the air or water, which is why these are so strictly regulated. Land contamination is a problem, but the pathway to the final receptor is usually groundwater. Generally the following types of incidents cause pollution:

- loss of containment, e.g. mechanical failure of tanks and pipes;
- fire;
- explosion;

- human error, e.g. leaving valves open, putting the wrong material in the wrong place;
- deliberate damage, e.g. vandalism, sabotage or terrorism.

Definition of risk

As we saw in Chapter 3, the standard definition of risk is:

Risk = probability of an impact happening x severity of that impact

As discussed in Chapter 3, it is dangerous to rely solely on this definition of risk as the public, press and your customers will see a high severity/low probability risk as much worse than high probability/low severity risks. You should take this perception into account when classifying risks, i.e. you should take those high severity risks more seriously internally.

Risk identification methods

There is a large number of formal risk identification methods including:

- Hazard and Operability (HAZOP) analysis: a structured brainstorming method designed to identify every conceivable deviation from normal practice.[41] It is most frequently used in the chemical industry.
- Fault Tree Analysis (FTA): a 'top down' approach to risk identification particularly suitable for large complex products.
- Failure Mode Cause & Effect Analysis (FMCEA): a bottom up approach which identifies potential failures at a component level and how they might affect the overall system. It is more rigorous, and thus more labour intensive, than FTA, so it is suitable for highly safety critical applications.

Resources with further information on these methods can be seen in Appendix 1.

Risk management

Given the definition of risk, there are two ways of decreasing risk:

1   Decreasing probability by ensuring that the system is designed to minimize risk and that staff are trained appropriately
2   Decreasing impact if that risk does occur, e.g. by ensuring bunds, spill kits and emergency procedures etc. are in place.

Some generic top tips follow to help you manage risks.

Top ten tips to avoid pollution incidences

- Carry out risk assessments.
- Remove hazardous materials from your inventory wherever possible. This can be done by ordering 'a little but often', and by green procurement, cleaner production and eco-design.
- Design your process to minimize the opportunities for an incident happening (e.g. store the minimum possible amounts of hazardous materials on site and choose their location carefully).
- Keep well-maintained spill kits near any store of hazardous material.
- Train staff to deal with all spills immediately.
- Map and understand your on-site drainage. Make sure all drains are colour coded: blue for surface water and red for the sewer is a standard approach.
- Check bunds are water tight; people have a nasty habit of knocking a hole in the side to let rainwater out.
- Check that nozzles and pipes do not reach over the sides of bunds at ground level – a passing vehicle could knock them off.
- Walk your site regularly and have a zero tolerance for unsafe working practices and bodges, such as machinery missing guards, or tools left near moving parts.
- Make being responsible for a pollution incident through negligence a disciplinary offence.

Waste Minimization and Recycling

The true cost of waste

The true cost of waste to a business has been estimated to be between 5 and 20 times its disposal cost.[42] This is because the true cost includes:

- the cost of raw materials;
- the cost of auxiliary materials;
- the cost of labour;
- the cost of energy;
- the opportunity cost of not selling wasted product;
- the cost of disposal.

The true cost of waste tends to increase as you move from goods in to goods out (see Figure 4.1). On more than one occasion, for example, I have witnessed packing machines spewing high value pharmaceutical products across the floor. In each case, the production manager didn't seem too bothered by the fact that the source of the company's profit was being lost after all that effort creating it.

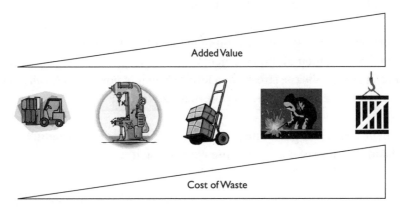

Figure 4.1 The relationship between added value and the cost of waste

Waste hierarchy

One of the most widely used tools for eco-efficiency is the waste hierarchy (see Figure 4.2). This sets out waste management options in order of preference, with the avoidance of waste in the first place being the ultimate goal.

Figure 4.2 The waste hierarchy

Most people treat the waste hierarchy as if it is carved in stone, but it is a simple rule of thumb and is not based on any rigorous scientific or economic analysis. There are two drawbacks of the hierarchy:

1   It does not encourage substitution of materials, so its use is ultimately limited to incremental improvements.
2   You can reduce a waste stream to a level where it is not economically viable to recycle and end up landfilling the material instead.

So, while it is a useful guideline, it is not an immutable law of nature and you should add in a dose of common sense while using it.

Waste minimization

Waste minimization is about avoiding waste occurring in the first place. The basic model of a waste minimization process is:

- map out your process and identify where waste occurs;
- calculate in theory how much of each type of waste should arise in each case, for example using a mass balance (what goes in to the process has to come out somewhere);
- measure how much waste actually arises at each point;
- check whether this correlates with the total amount of waste disposal you pay for;
- estimate the true cost to your organization of all waste (see 'The true cost of waste' on p81);
- carry out a walkover review to identify anomalies, poor performance and 'quick win' solutions – see top tips below for help;
- draw up a priority list of waste using cost as a guide;
- for each item, determine the root cause of that waste arising;
- develop action plans to address those root causes.

This process should be integrated into your environmental management system (if you have one) (see p45).

Reuse and recycling

The terms reuse and recycling are often used interchangeably, but strictly speaking they are different:

- Reuse is when a material or item is be used again in its current form, with or without a small amount of repair
- Recycling is when material is recovered and used to manufacture a new product.

For example, if a pallet is used again as a pallet, that is reuse, but if it is chipped to make chipboard, then it has been recycled.

Recycling and reuse have two main environmental benefits:

1   Keeping material out of landfill. Landfill space is scarce in many countries. Organic material decomposes in landfill to produce a 50:50 mix of carbon dioxide and methane, the latter being a powerful greenhouse gas. Also toxic materials can leach out of landfills and contaminate groundwater.
2   Avoiding material extraction. As we saw in Chapter 1, primary industries tend to be the most environmentally damaging, so by providing relatively 'clean' material, those 'dirty' processes can be avoided, for example recycling 1kg of aluminium only requires 9 per cent of the energy of extracting material from ore.

Reuse opportunities

According to the waste hierarchy, reuse is preferable to recycling, but the main obstacle is matching the amount of material generated with the reuse opportunity. For example, it is often possible to use some packaging from 'goods in' for storing materials or work in progress on site, but it is rare that this use will require more than a minimal amount. A better option is to return used packaging to the supplier to be reused for their original purpose and indeed some pallet supply companies insist on this.

In an office environment, a policy of reusing furniture, filing containers and even envelopes can make a real difference to waste arisings, but require effective staff engagement to make sure it happens on the ground.

Recycling

There are two forms of recycling:

1   Internal recycling: for example the chipboard manufacturer Egger recycles off-spec product back into their process or uses it for fuel.[43]
2   External recycling: transferring the material to another organization to reprocess the material.

In both cases it is important to ensure that recycling does not mask a deeper problem. For instance I was called into a factory where the environmental manager boasted that he had an 80 per cent recycling rate and the cost of the service was less than the cost of landfill. When I dug a little deeper I found that a lot of that material was still being wasted unnecessarily. By explaining the true cost of waste he was persuaded that some drastic waste minimization was required. We also managed to persuade one supplier to change their packaging so it could be recycled rather than landfilled, thus improving on his impressive recycling figures.

The need for segregation of material for recycling depends on the materials and the capability of your reprocessor(s). Some reprocessors will take mixed waste and segregate it themselves, others will require clean material streams. If you need to do the segregation, then a consistent colour coding scheme will help your staff find the right bin for each waste. While there is no universal colour coding convention, some sectors have their own system, for example the UK construction industry[44] which uses white bins for gypsum rich material (e.g. wall boards), blue bins for metals and orange bins for hazardous waste etc.

Careful positioning of bins will encourage recycling. For example, to encourage paper recycling in an office, replace each waste bin with a paper recycling bin and provide a single general waste bin, say, at the end of each corridor.

From a sustainability point of view, the eventual fate of your material is very important. As we saw in Chapter 2, a dominance of 'downcycling' (using material for a lower grade purpose than its original use) will compromise the 'cyclic' principle of 'Solar, Cyclic, Safe'. Materials should be recycled into a similar use or 'upcycled' to a higher grade use. New technology is helping this, for example, it is now possible to recycle plastic drinks bottles back into plastic drinks bottles whereas previously for food safety reasons they had to be down-cycled into lower grade uses (e.g. fleeces, bollards).[45]

Top ten tips for offices

- Set all printers and photocopiers to double-sided printing as a default where available. Install a print auditing system to identify use patterns.
- Provide all internal documentation in electronic format and use electronic media for invitations and registration for meetings, conferences etc.
- Replace each waste bin with a paper recycling bin and provide a single general waste bin, say, at the end of each corridor.

- Replace meeting handouts with digital presentations. Make the presentations available on-line instead.
- Plan food for meetings carefully, and let other staff know when there might be leftovers.
- Keep a tight control on ordering stationery.
- Encourage staff to reuse folders, box files, etc.
- Use multi-use envelopes for internal mail and restrict the supply so staff have to reuse them.
- Discourage the production of epic reports. Proctor and Gamble have a 'one page memo' policy to encourage concise communications – it will cut paper waste too.
- Avoid disposable crockery and cutlery.

Top ten tips for factories

- Get all your staff involved in the process: they will know where waste occurs better than you.
- Provide separate, distinctive bins or skips (different colours are better than relying on labels) for recyclable materials.
- Pay careful attention to packaging and dispatch areas. This is where waste causes most financial and environmental harm as your product has highest added value.
- Ask suppliers to minimize or to take back packaging, or at least to design it for easy recycling.
- Reuse packaging internally, e.g. pallets and cartons.
- Carry out maintenance checks on machinery on a regular basis. Annual checks should be the minimum.
- Keep a tight control on stores to avoid casual overuse of materials.
- Design your product to minimize waste.
- Make your packaging appropriate to protect your product.
- Avoid over-ordering raw materials, lubricants, spares etc.

Energy Efficiency

Energy, cost and carbon

Unlike the cost of waste, much of which is hidden like an iceberg, energy costs are easier to measure and are high enough to have a significant impact on most businesses. Fortunately energy efficiency gains are relatively easy to identify and address, and the measures required tend to pay for themselves very quickly.

Don't forget that, in carbon terms, not all energy is equal:

- Gas and oil are relatively cheap and have a low carbon intensity (kg carbon dioxide per unit energy).
- Mains electricity is more expensive and has a much higher carbon intensity.
- Compressed air is the most expensive form of energy on most industrial sites as it is produced inefficiently from electricity. Therefore it also has the highest carbon intensity.

Many people mix up electricity and energy (just watch the media for daily examples), but it is important to make the distinction.

Energy auditing

Energy auditing is usually easier than waste auditing as your energy bill(s) are a ready-made record of consumption. The steps are:

- Map your process(es) and identify where energy is used. If you have carried out a carbon footprinting exercise you will already have the high level information to start this exercise.
- Check whether this correlates with the total amount of consumption on your bills.

- Carry out a walkover review of the facility to identify anomalies, poor performance and 'quick win solutions' – see top tips below for help.
- Engage with your staff to identify more saving opportunities.
- Draw up a priority list of energy efficiency measures using cost as a guide.
- Develop action plans to improve energy efficiency.

Some additional diagnostic tips are:

- If your business does not work around the clock, check what the overnight/downtime consumption is. Reductions in this 'baseload' are usually the most cost effective.
- Each month plot the average energy consumption for the previous 12 months to spot upward or downward trends (the 12-month scope will account for seasonal variations).
- In particular, check that heating fuel costs drop off in the spring. If they don't, your heating hasn't been adjusted to the warmer temperatures and your staff are probably opening their windows to compensate.
- You can use 'degree days' to make a more robust check on space heating requirements. The number of 'degree days' in a month is a measure of the severity of cold weather – check out the Carbon Trust website for a description of how to use them.[46]
- If you use a lot of compressed air then ultrasonic compressed air leak detectors can pay for themselves very quickly.

Top ten tips for offices

Unlike housing where heating dominates, the main problem for modern offices is cooling. Offices with air conditioning have double the carbon footprint of those without.[47] Some energy efficiency tips are:

- Run a 'Switch it off' campaign. Rebut energy myths like 'it is more efficient to leave lights on than to switch them on and off'.
- Provide feedback to your staff on energy consumption. Switch it off campaigns work best with real data to back up the message.

- Purchase office equipment that meets a recognized energy efficiency standard (e.g. EnergyStar, Energy Savings Trust).
- Upgrade all lighting to the most energy efficient models.
- Reduce the level of lighting in non-critical areas. Most corridors are much brighter than they need to be.
- Install automatic lighting controls, particularly for windowless rooms.
- Set heating controls to the optimum temperature and make sure they remain there.
- Make sure your heating tracks the temperature outside in the spring and autumn. If staff start opening the windows to ventilate rooms, then energy is being wasted.
- In larger organizations, install a tea urn rather than individual kettles.
- Laptop batteries will discharge if you leave them plugged into the wall, whether or not the plug is switched on – unplug them to save the charge.

Top ten tips for factories

- Launch a 'Switch it off' campaign: calculate how much money your business is paying for energy and display this with the message.
- Install curtains at all entrances and exits.
- Zone heating and lighting systems so they can be adjusted to shift patterns – there is no point in heating the entire factory just so one person can supervise weekend deliveries.
- Check your air compressor is installed correctly and takes its air intake from outside. I have seen many compressors effectively sucking in their own hot exhaust – this is very inefficient.
- Check for compressed air leaks. It has been estimated that a pin-sized hole will cost £600 per annum on energy costs. Walk around in downtime to hear leaks or invest in an ultrasonic detector.
- Identify opportunities for waste heat recovery, such as capturing hot air and/or hot water from compressors. The heat can be used for space heating or to heat water for hand-washing and cleaning.
- Make sure cold room and refrigerator doors are alarmed so staff are alerted if they are left open.

- Implement an upgrade plan for motors, and always buy the most efficient model as any additional cost will be paid back very quickly in most cases.
- Install variable speed drive motors where appropriate, e.g. rather than constantly pumping a fluid against a valve.
- Make sure all hot water pipes and fittings are adequately lagged.

Water Conservation

Water, water, everywhere

When I do site audits with companies, it is perfectly normal to come across a hose left running with its free end stuck into a drain. At this point the site manager or whoever is accompanying me suggests that this is a one-off and I shouldn't really worry about it in my report. I always make a point of flagging it up as water is one area where industry can really shape up.

One of the problems with water is that there is a persistent myth that it is free. Envirowise estimates[48] that in the UK:

- Every cubic metre (1000 litres) of water costs £1.20 in supply and sewage treatment charges.
- A two-drop per second leak will cost £16 per annum in water and sewerage costs.
- A 5mm stream of water will cost £900 per annum.

Water bills

Water is becoming an increasingly precious and therefore expensive resource. In addition, tighter requirements on waste water treatment have increased disposal costs as well.

In the UK, sewage costs are set using the Mogden formula. This calculates the price for each unit of water using the following factors:

- basic treatment cost;
- Suspended Solids (SS): cloudiness in layman's terms;
- Chemical Oxygen Demand (COD): this is the amount of oxygen required to break down the organic material (and other pollutants that absorb oxygen) in the effluent.

As this is a per volume cost, simply diluting your effluent may keep you within limits for SS or COD, but it will *not* reduce your costs under the formula – this is a common misconception. If you dispose of a significant amount of fat to sewer, for example in the food production or catering businesses, a skimmer and/or a microbial treatment system will cut the COD part of the charges significantly.

Water auditing

The process for water auditing is very similar to that for waste and energy. The steps are:

- develop a map of your site or process, plotting where water enters and leaves;
- create a water balance to show how much water comes on site and where it goes;
- compare water bills to this model and identify any discrepancies;
- carry out a walkover review of the facility to identify anomalies, poor performance and 'quick win solutions' – see top tips below for help;
- draw up a priority list of water conservation measures using cost as a guide;
- develop action plans to reduce water usage.

Some auditing tips are:

- If you do not operate around the clock, check what the overnight/downtime consumption is. This can often detect leaks and other problems.
- If you have a large site with an old water supply then leaks can be very difficult to detect. Use an ultrasonic leak detector to locate them (a number of companies offer this service).

Top five tips for offices

- Install percussion (push) taps on all wash hand basins. This can cut water use by 50 per cent.
- Install waterless urinals and low flush toilets.
- Purchase water-conserving dishwashing machines and other white goods.

- Make sure there is a system for fixing leaks as soon as they are reported.
- Install a rainwater harvesting system for flushing toilets if space permits.

Top five tips for factories

- Fix all leaks and overflows immediately.
- Install trigger nozzles on all hoses.
- Use a brush to sweep up slurries rather than using a hose.
- Use rainwater for low-grade water use like yard cleaning.
- Cascade water from high purity uses to lower grade uses (e.g. using 'last rinse' water for the next 'first wash').

Greening Your Supply Chain

Don't buy trouble

A relatively easy way to improve the environmental performance of your company is to make it policy to buy environmentally friendly products and services. This avoids problems at your end as you aren't buying, say, hazardous materials, and it also strengthens markets for green products.

Green procurement is synonymous with lengthy supplier questionnaires, but I'm convinced that the process doesn't need to be complicated to be effective.

You have the following options to green your supply chain:

- purchase less product;
- purchase 'better' products;
- purchase services rather than products;
- purchase from 'better' suppliers: i.e. those who have a better environmental performance;
- engage your supply chain to find win-win solutions.

The sections below describe each of these in turn.

Purchasing less product

Over-purchasing goods, particularly those with a limited shelf life, is a prime cause of 'hidden' waste. Buying material simply to throw it away is bad business.

I worked with a client in the construction industry who was purchasing standard length pieces of timber, then cutting them to size on site. In other words he was taking material on site simply to remove it. At my suggestion he started buying the timber at the size he needed and immediately cut his waste costs and saved on the cutting time. As a bonus he could also get the back doors of his van shut with the shorter wood – much appreciated in the winter.

A month or two later I was visiting a manufacturer of bespoke large electrical equipment enclosures. They were taking the steel angles that made up the frame of the enclosure and cutting them every time. I noted that the off-cuts were always the same size and suggested they see if their supplier could provide the angles at the length they required. They could and it saved them money on raw material costs, cutting costs and waste costs.

You and your staff should always ask the following questions of procurement decisions:

- Do we need it?
- Can we do with less?
- Can we buy it in quantities that better match our needs?
- Will we use it within its shelf life?

Purchasing 'better' products

What is an environmentally friendly product?

This will be discussed in much more detail in the eco-design section in Chapter 5, but in line with our strategy from Chapter 2, we will define it as one that is:

- Solar, Cyclic, Safe, and/or
- eco-efficient with a target of factor 10.

When I do training courses on green products, I use a simple matrix to compare the 'green' option against the standard product. This allows the environmental performance to be judged very quickly: if you can't spot a benefit with this system, then it probably isn't significant.

Table 4.1 *Green purchasing matrix*

Product	Solar	Cyclic	Safe	Efficient
Recycled paper		✔ ✔		✔
Compact fluorescent light bulbs			✗	✔ ✔

Where: ✔ ✔ signifies much better performance
    ✔ signifies a better performance
    ✗ signifies worse performance

So in our example, buying fluorescent light bulbs gives a significantly better performance in energy efficiency, but at the expense of containing a toxic material.

Black and grey lists

Many companies use 'black' and 'grey' lists to filter out materials and chemicals which are not 'safe', for example the car manufacturer Volvo. Black list substances should never be purchased and those on the grey list should only be used where no alternative exits.

Black and grey lists are highly industry specific, so you will need to research toxic materials in your business and determine which can and can't be replaced.

Other issues

The matrix above gives you a quick and dirty method of judging the product, but you will need to consider a number of other issues, for example:

- Where does the product come from?
- How far does it travel to get to your premises?
- Are there any ethical concerns about the product or its manufacturer?
- How is the product packaged?

Buying a service rather than a product

One of the most powerful methods of reducing the impact of your procurement is to buy services rather than products. For example Xerox do not sell photo-copiers, rather it provides a copying service. Its machines have been developed to be long-lasting and easily upgradeable. You pay per copy you make, which discourages you from being wasteful.

The idea of the product service system is described in more detail in Chapter 5 as an option for your own business model, but the system can be used for purchasing as well.

Purchasing from 'better' suppliers

The press, NGOs, clients and customers and the general public will hold you responsible for the performance of your suppliers. This has been particularly noticeable in the human rights field (e.g. sweat shops producing clothing), but environmental problems in the supply chain can also embarrass high profile businesses.

For example, the Toyota Prius has been attacked because the nickel required for its battery comes from a smelter in Sudbury, Canada, which has had pollution problems in the past. Never mind that the ecological damage was caused decades before the Prius ever went on sale, or that the factory has won awards for restoration since; Toyota has been unfairly tarred with this brush.

For this reason if you are going to present yourself as a green business you need to be careful about who you do business with, and indeed who they do business with.

There are a number of ways to identify potential problems:

- keep an eye on the environmental press, both at the business end of the market (e.g. the environmental trade journal, the *ENDS Report*) and the activist end (e.g. *New Internationalist*);
- there are many books and reports available that list the 'ethical' performance of companies against set criteria;
- audit potential suppliers using short supplier questionnaires and visit their main sites if possible.

Engaging your supply chain to find win–win solutions

All the above solutions take a command and control approach to greening your supply chain. But good solutions to environmental problems can be found by working with your suppliers to develop win–win solutions.

For example:

- better matching of dimensions and/or quantities;
- avoiding adding features or treatments that you do not need;

- developing more eco-friendly components as a joint research and development (R&D) venture;
- reusable packaging and the necessary reverse logistics system to return it to the supplier.

Top ten tips for green procurement

- Buy less stuff, or buy better stuff.
- Eliminate what you don't need.
- Order quantities to closely match your needs.
- Minimize the use of lengthy supplier questionnaires – keep them short and to the point.
- Buy services rather than products where possible.
- Analyse options using the Solar, Cyclic, Safe, efficient criteria.
- Work with your suppliers to match specification to your needs.
- Work with your suppliers to optimize packaging.
- Research suppliers' backgrounds to ensure you will not get blamed for their sins.
- Draw up black and grey lists to screen out toxic materials.

Transport

Overview

Moving people and goods uses about a quarter of all the energy consumed in the UK. It follows that transport contributes a major part of the environmental impact of most companies, whether it is logistics, work journeys or staff commuting to and from your sites. Table 4.2 below gives figures for the carbon intensity (the amount of carbon dioxide produced per passenger per kilometre) for various modes of transport.

Green travel plan

Green travel plans were originally introduced to reduce the number of employees commuting to work in individual cars, but it is worth developing a plan to cover all transport as it is interrelated. For example, if a staff member

Table 4.2 *Carbon intensity of different forms of transport*[49]

Mode	kg CO_2 per passenger per km
Average petrol car (driver only)	0.21
Domestic flight	0.18
Bus	0.10
Motorcycle	0.09
Underground travel	0.07
Rail	0.06
Bike	0.00*
Foot	0.00*

Note: * These figures exclude the carbon emitted to produce the food required for extra calories burnt in these modes of transport.

arrives by bus, but needs to visit a remote site, they will need an appropriate form of transport.

There are many incentives to develop a green travel plan. The UK's Department for Transport (DfT) found that the average annual cost of maintaining a parking space is £300–£500 while the cost of running a plan was £47 per employee per year.[50] Many local authorities will insist on a green travel plan for large developments as part of planning permission.

The planning process usually is a variation on the following:

- survey staff members to determine where they live and how they get to work;
- gather information on official work journeys whether they start from your premises or from employees' homes;
- plot staff journeys on a map or a Graphical Information System (GIS);
- identify opportunities to reduce single occupation car use.

Some potential solutions are:

- limiting parking permits: a fair and transparent method of allocating permits based on need rather than seniority is required to avoid staff insurrection;
- paying extra to those who do not take a permit;
- charging daily parking charges can give staff more flexibility than permits. For example an employee may use the bus most days, but needs to use a car one day a week for the school run;
- identifying and addressing 'missing links' in local transport provision, e.g. negotiating changes to bus services or providing cycle access to and from major cycle routes;
- subsidizing public transport costs;
- working in collaboration with other local employers to share the cost of, for example, new bus routes.

Producing a green travel plan is not a trivial task and I would recommend getting in some expert help. There are many consultants who are highly skilled in doing this effectively.

Unnecessary transport emissions

Once, in my youth, I was taken half way across the country by a more senior colleague, put up in a hotel for the night and taken out for a curry, all for a half hour meeting the next day. On the way back, he freely admitted that he called the meeting to get the overnight stay and dinner on the firm. This was a blatant waste of money and fuel, and this kind of behaviour is all too common.

The following tips can help reduce unnecessary transport emissions:

- Make sure your travel and subsistence rules do not encourage staff to go on 'jollies'.
- Use telephone or video conferencing where possible.
- Train staff in eco-friendly driving techniques (avoiding hard acceleration and braking).
- For freight, practice 'back-loading' where possible. This is the art of making sure a goods vehicle never travels empty.
- Put trackers on fleet vehicles – this can lead to dramatic cuts in fuel consumption by eliminating unauthorized trips.
- Provide high-quality, covered, secure cycle parking close to your building/premises.
- Provide showers and lockers for cyclists.

More efficient means of transport

Vehicles can be made more efficient by either reducing weight, aerodynamic drag or by building more efficient engines. The Toyota Prius hybrid does all three – it is light, very aerodynamic and it has a small petrol engine, helped out at slow speeds by an electric motor. Even the brakes help charge the battery by converting the energy of the car's movement into electrical energy.

Electric vehicles are becoming more common – in environmental terms, they tend to be best for short start/stop journeys such as local delivery services.

In terms of conventional vehicles:

- Smaller vehicles are generally more fuel efficient than their larger equivalents.

- Diesel engines do more miles to the gallon than their petrol equivalents, but produce more lung-damaging particulates. This is a difficult trade-off to make.

Alternative fuels

The most popular way of using renewable energy in transport is the use of biofuels like bioethanol and biodiesel. Bioethanol is alcohol fermented from sugars and is popular in Brazil. Biodiesel is made from plant oils or waste vegetable oil. It is normally blended with normal fossil fuel diesel. The most common blend is known as B5 which is 5 per cent biodiesel and 95 per cent diesel, although B20 (20 per cent biodiesel) is becoming more available.

Unfortunately there is not enough agricultural land to produce enough fuel crops to supply all today's cars with 100 per cent biofuel and the increasing popularity of biofuels has been blamed for the loss of rainforest and soaring food prices. Second generation biofuels are made from agricultural by-products so are less harmful in this respect. Third generation biofuels are produced by algae and hold much promise but are still under development. In the meantime, if you do use biofuel then make sure it does come from a sustainable source.

One method that is being developed is to use an energy store such as electricity or hydrogen to allow renewable energy generated from other sources to power vehicles. At the time of writing, electric vehicles are experiencing a mini-boom. Hydrogen technology is too immature to consider, but may be a solution in the longer term.

Telecommuting/teleworking

The number of people working from home, also known as telecommuting or tele-working, has increased steadily over recent years as technology improves and as the UK economy continues shifting from manufacturing towards a knowledge-based economy. There are two potential environmental benefits to teleworking:

1 reduction in carbon dioxide, air pollutants and congestion from commuting;
2 reduction in carbon dioxide from carbon-intensive office accommodation.

In terms of the former, there have been concerns that the benefits of reducing commuter journeys may be offset by generating other journeys such as those which would have been combined with the commute or by freeing up cars for other family members. An analysis of teleworking research commissioned by the UK's DfT[51] found no empirical evidence for this rebound.

The DfT report estimated that teleworkers reduce their mileage by 48 to 77 per cent on teleworking days and 11 to 19 per cent overall. There was also evidence of a 'contracted action space' amongst those working from home – in other words teleworkers tend to use amenities closer to home. The report also concluded that 22 to 40 per cent of the UK's labour force could telework to some extent.

Office accommodation is very carbon intensive. The average office worker is responsible for 1.3–1.5 tonnes of CO_2 every year while at work compared to the average 1.2 tonnes of CO_2 for the average person from domestic heating.[52] While some of the heating requirement will shift from the office to teleworkers' homes during the winter, there is still likely to be a significant CO_2 saving. It has been estimated that giving staff the opportunity to work from home two days per week can reduce the requirement for office space (with its attendant heating, ventilation and/or air conditioning – HVAC) by approximately 20 per cent.

Top ten tips for greening transport

- Produce a green travel plan.
- Rationalize parking to encourage other forms of commuting.
- Provide bicycle racks, lockers and showers.
- Negotiate with public transport providers to optimize routes.
- Hire or purchase efficient vehicles.
- Use alternative (low carbon) fuels.
- Train staff on fuel efficient driving techniques.
- Discourage unnecessary travel through teleconferencing and back-loading of freight.
- Eliminate unauthorized travel.
- Encourage telecommuting.

Carbon Offsetting

What is carbon offsetting?

Carbon offsetting is the idea of buying 'carbon credits' to balance the amount of carbon dioxide you produce. Your money is invested in low carbon projects such as renewable energy, energy efficiency or, most controversially, tree planting. Alternatively it is used to buy up carbon credits in carbon trading schemes to limit further the amount of carbon that can be emitted by participants within the scheme.

Controversy

The concept of offsetting is highly controversial with some commentators even likening it to the medieval European custom of buying absolution for crimes such as incest.[53] Others have criticized the effectiveness of the offsetting projects and there is a huge argument over the concept of *additionality*: whether the carbon cuts you are paying for would have happened anyway.

The additionality argument works like this. Various bodies including the governments and large energy companies are committed to making cuts in carbon emissions under agreements such as the Kyoto protocol and national energy efficiency legislation. Therefore if you pay for cuts in this country, you are contributing to their commitment which they would have had to do anyway. This argument has effectively pushed offsetting projects overseas to non-Kyoto countries where it is more difficult to monitor their effectiveness. It also opens up the moral argument of whether we're paying the poor to cut their energy use so we can continue polluting.

My view

I believe that a carbon offset operates like a voluntary carbon tax which is ring-fenced for low carbon projects. The very people who criticize the morality of offsetting would agree to such a carbon tax if it was compulsory, so what is so wrong with a voluntary tax?

I also believe the additionality argument is overstated. That logic suggests that nobody living in a Kyoto country should make any behavioural changes or invest in any low carbon technology, but rather wait for the government to sort it all out for us. That is clearly nonsense. If offsetting can contribute to the Kyoto commitment then great – we should be proud to contribute to our national targets. They are *our* targets, not just the government's.

The effectiveness of tree planting to absorb carbon is controversial, but not even the strongest critics can deny that a well-designed and maintained scheme is environmentally beneficial. In any case, tree planting is rarely part of the equation in modern offsetting schemes.

How does offsetting work?

If you decide to go down the offsetting path you must ensure that your carbon offsetting is not used as a way of 'doing nothing', but as the final part of a three part process:

1   measure your carbon footprint (see chapter 3);
2   reduce carbon emissions where possible;
3   offset the remainder.

There are a number of different kinds of offset scheme:

●   voluntary projects, some of whom sign up for one of a variety of quality protocols. Example projects include community renewables, insulating fuel poor homes, providing energy efficient equipment to the public and tree planting (to 'sequester' carbon);
●   credits from certified sources, such as projects certified by the Kyoto Clean Development Mechanism (CDM) or the Kyoto Joint Implementation Mechanism. These are probably the most robust form of offset, as they are closely monitored;

- purchasing allowances from 'cap and trade' schemes such as the European Union Emissions Trading Scheme and 'retiring' them (i.e. tearing them up) so the companies in the scheme will be forced to collectively cut their emissions by that amount.

Choosing an offset scheme

If you buy an offset, you want to know that the process actually delivers the carbon cuts you are buying. This means that the offset is effective *and* additional (to a level which you are happy with).

Effectiveness

To ensure the effectiveness of an offset scheme, there are three questions you need to ask and I'll illustrate them using tree planting:

1 technical effectiveness: does the offset project actually cut carbon, and, if so, how much? For example: how much carbon do trees sequester? (The answer depends on local conditions);
2 rebound effects (or 'leakage'): will the project inadvertently cause an emissions increase elsewhere? For example, will the tree planting process release carbon from the soil? (It can do, it depends on the soil.) Or would the tree planting in one area lead to tree felling elsewhere due to land use pressures? (More difficult to answer);
3 permanence: is the carbon removed forever? For example will the trees be cut down for fuel or development sometime in the future? (They would need legal protection).

Similar uncertainties will apply to any offset project and you will have to ensure that they have been minimized as much as possible through good governance by the offsetting organization.

Additionality

This is the more complex issue. As I have stated above, on the one hand, I personally have no problem with an offset scheme that 'helps out' a Kyoto signatory country, but on the other hand, I would want to know that my offset is not letting a private sector company (e.g. an energy company) off the hook by contributing to its legal obligations to cut carbon (e.g. the UK Renewables Obligation – see p117). The killer questions to ask are:

● Will the carbon cut only happen if I buy this offset?
● Who else will benefit from this carbon cut?

Which scheme for you?

In terms of which type of scheme to go for, it is a matter of what suits you or your organization. If you simply want to offset your carbon in as robust a manner as possible and don't care about how it is actually done, then go for CDM-type schemes or purchase and retire allowances. If you see offsetting as more of a Corporate Social Responsibility (CSR)-type activity and that the investment in a specific project (e.g. a local project or one which also meets a societal need related to your sphere of business) is more important than the robustness of the offset, then find a voluntary scheme that suits you and do your homework on its effectiveness and additionality. Of course, you may have to loosen your additionality criteria or take a chance on effectiveness to get the project you want.

Chapter 5

Huge Leaps

Doing the Right Thing

Going green for a living

This is where it gets exciting. The radical concepts and examples in this section will get you out of your comfort zone and into true green innovation. Many of the strategies are medium- to high- risk so you will need to do your homework and weigh up the costs, benefits and risks before proceeding with any project, but the potential rewards are huge.

This chapter will affect your business in the following ways:

- changing your process: cleaner production;
- changing your supply chain: renewable energy and Industrial Symbiosis;
- changing your premises: eco-building;
- changing your product: eco-design;
- changing your business model: product service systems;
- exploiting synergies between the above.

Implementation

Strategy

This is where backcasting comes into its own. If you are going to change your business model, you will probably need to redesign your product. In turn, if you want to redesign your product, you will probably need to (or want to, given the opportunity) redesign your process and your supply chain. Putting all these together in the right order and avoiding conflicts can be difficult. Backcasting gives you a much better chance of getting it right first time.

Obstacles

You will face the following obstacles to implementing the solutions in this chapter:

- capital costs: changing your process and buildings will require a significant investment;
- disruption: radical changes will always involve disruption in your business processes which will have a knock on effect on your cash flow;
- immaturity of markets: will your customers buy your new product or service?
- immaturity of technology: will the technology you require be available at the scale and reliability you require?
- immaturity of supply chains: can your suppliers deliver? Are new suppliers reliable?

The key to overcoming or avoiding these obstacles is to bear in mind the caveat in Secret No 1: Don't forget you are still running a business. You will need to treat green innovation in the same way you would assess any other business investment.

Resources

Implementing solutions in this chapter will require more resources than your staff committee. I recommend time-limited action teams who will design, implement, and review each solution before disbanding. The following may be required:

- production engineers;
- design engineers;
- sales and marketing staff;
- financial staff;
- technical experts.

Some of these you may have in your company, but you may have to buy in the expertise you require.

Cleaner Production

A history of pollution prevention

The following is a potted history of approaches to pollution prevention through the centuries according to Professor Tim Jackson of Surrey University:[54]

- foul and flee: humans used whatever resources they could get their hands on and didn't worry about the consequences as the world was big enough to move somewhere else;
- dilute and disperse: the introduction of sewage systems and factories with chimneys meant that pollution could be diluted in the air and water to a level which, those responsible hoped, caused no significant human health problems;
- concentrate and contain (also known as 'end of pipe abatement'): equipment was developed to start capturing and/or treating pollution, for example electrostatic or bag filters on chimneys, chemical/biological treatment of effluent, catalytic converters on cars etc;
- cleaner production: the fourth and latest stage of this evolution. This involves the redesign of manufacturing systems to avoid pollution before it occurs.

The first two of these are outdated and largely illegal in industrialized countries. End of pipe systems are generally undesirable, as they add cost to the manufacturing process and often reduce the efficiency of the process they are cleaning up. By shifting to cleaner production, pollution is reduced for free by avoiding it in the first place – once you have paid off the capital costs.

While cleaner production can be introduced into a facility gradually, it is more cost effective to incorporate it into new facilities or during major upgrades.

Cleaner production techniques

Cleaner production tends to be industry-specific, for example:

- the use of membrane technology in the chlorine industry;
- using electrolytic smelting instead of thermal smelting in the metal industries;
- water based printing technologies;
- lead free soldering systems in electronics.

The following general techniques can be applied across a range of sectors:

- Straightening pipework: pushing fluids around 90° corners takes a huge amount of energy yet we tend to build spaghetti-like process plants. Straightening pipework can vastly reduce pumping costs.
- Waste heat recovery: waste heat from a number of sources can be used to heat water, air or reactants.
- Invest in efficient motors and installing variable speed drives in pumps rather than using energy to push fluids against a valve.

These examples are all from the manufacturing sector where the idea of cleaner production is most common. However there is nothing to stop other industries changing their business processes to align themselves to sustainability principles, for example:

- a logistics company may adopt smarter routing and reusable packaging;
- modern road construction techniques avoid the need to remove large amounts of the existing roadway, recycling what is removed back into the new surface;
- no-dig cable installation.

The future of cleaner production

There are a number of novel technologies which hold the promise of a massively reduced environmental impact. Again these are highly sector specific, but some examples are listed below.

Process intensification

The idea of 'small is beautiful' in the chemical industry emerged from ICI in the 1970s. Process intensification was defined as a 'reduction in plant size by at least a factor 100'. While this is still an ambition, its proponents claim that they have, for example, reduced the energy requirements for certain processes by 70 per cent in practice.[55]

Nanotechnology

Nanotechnology involves technology working at the scale of nanometres (1×10^{-9}m). There have been a number of environmental concerns over the implications of nanotechnology ranging from the health effects of tiny particles to sci-fi type scares of grey goo or nanorobots taking over the world. However, nanotechnology is additive (building materials from their component parts) compared to our usual subtractive manufacturing processes (starting with a large amount of material and cutting it to shape) so could deliver true zero waste manufacturing.

Current applications involve 'first generation' passive nanomaterials, for example:

- titanium dioxide nanoparticles in sunscreen, cosmetics and food products;
- silver nanoparticles in food packaging, clothing, disinfectants and household appliances;
- zinc oxide nanoparticles in sunscreens and cosmetics, surface coatings, paints and outdoor furniture varnishes.

The future is in 'second generation' active nanoparticles – so watch out for the grey goo.

Bio-processing

Bio-processing uses micro-organisms ('bugs') or enzymes to do the hard work of chemical and materials production. Biological processes tend to work at moderate temperatures and pressures unlike traditional chemical production. They also have to avoid many toxic chemicals to avoid poisoning the bugs. Applications include food, animal feed, pharmaceuticals, chemicals, plastics (bio-plastics) and paper.

Supercritical fluids

A material becomes supercritical at temperatures and pressures above its thermo-dynamic critical point. Supercritical fluids (usually water and carbon dioxide) can replace toxic organic solvents in a range of industrial and laboratory processes, including:

- dry cleaning: replacing toxic solvents;
- dyeing: avoiding solvent based dyes;
- biodiesel production: raises the tolerance of the process to contaminants making the use of, say, waste cooking oils easier;
- Carbon Capture and Storage (CCS): provides a use for the carbon dioxide;
- refrigeration: supercritical carbon dioxide can replace other refrigerants which have a much higher climate change impact.

How to pursue cleaner production

As I mentioned above, cleaner production is very sector-dependent, so it is difficult to give any specific advice. However the following may help:

- Adopt an 'invest to save mentality', in other words, be prepared to cover higher capital costs to get lower operational costs. You may have to go into battle with your finance department to deliver this.
- Consult your sector organizations and publications to keep abreast of best practice. Engage with universities and other research bodies to identify and develop novel opportunities.
- Look at other sectors: most 'inventions' are actually the application of existing technology to uses where they haven't been tried before (e.g. the vortex in a Dyson vacuum cleaner was standard practice in industrial air filters before James Dyson tried it in a domestic application).

Note that the design of your product or service will be the most influential factor on your process. This will be discussed in later sections.

Top ten tips for cleaner production

- Forget 'how you've always done things'.
- Adopt an 'invest to save' culture.
- Plot your production process and engage your staff on potential solutions.
- Use 'The Toddler Test' – for each part of the process keep asking 'Why?' to determine whether an element is needed or being carried out in the best way.
- Consult your sector organizations and publications to keep abreast of best practice.
- Look at other sectors and cross fertilize ideas.
- Engage with universities and other research bodies.
- Use the resources listed in Appendix 1 to identify possible solutions.
- Carry out rigorous risk analyses of new technologies.
- Watch out for snake oil salesmen trying to sell ineffective or immature technologies.

Renewable Energy

Why?

As discussed in Chapter 1, energy is not only the lifeblood of the modern economy but also a major cause of climate change. In Chapter 2 we saw that the 'Solar' part of 'Solar, Cyclic, Safe' means that we should be shifting to 100 per cent renewable energy, but also that energy is the theoretical limiting factor in the ecological model of sustainability. Unfortunately, renewable energy is much more difficult to harness than fossil fuels, therefore it is imperative to drive down demand before starting to install renewables (see the section on energy efficiency in Chapter 4, p87).

(As an aside, I don't like the term 'renewable energy' as I don't think it means anything – only biomass energy is strictly 'renewable', the others are 'undepletable' – but it has entered the general lexicon, so we're stuck with it.)

Remember again not to confuse the terms 'electricity' and 'energy'. Mains electricity has a much higher carbon intensity than fossil fuels.

UK electricity production

A ROCky road

In the UK, the government has introduced the 'Renewables Obligation' to promote the introduction of renewable technologies. The obligation requires large energy providers to either produce a certain proportion of their electricity from renewables, or, buy Renewable Obligation Certificates (ROCs) from small renewable energy generators.

While the ROC system has undoubtedly helped smaller generators enter the market, environmental purists rate renewable electricity where the ROCs have been sold as 'less green' than electricity where the ROCs have been 'retired', i.e., torn up. This is because the large generators would have to produce the renewable energy themselves if the small generator didn't sell them the ROCs. This is a similar 'additionality' argument to that in the carbon offsetting debate discussed in Chapter 4.

Purchasing green electricity

The easiest way to get hold of green electricity is to purchase it from an external supplier. The idea of these suppliers is they ensure that the amount of energy you use is balanced by renewable energy being transmitted onto the grid. You don't necessarily get 'green electrons' yourself, but someone does!

The key issue in the UK is what happens to the ROCs. The greenest providers retire some or all of their ROCs, but most sell ROCs as part of their business model (this is also true of domestic green energy schemes). You will have to decide how green you want to be and choose appropriately.

Be wary of some 'green electricity' schemes which simply invest in developing new renewables schemes, rather than ensuring a green supply to match your consumption.

Some companies will install a wind turbine free of charge on your land and then sell you the electricity over a number of years. This is very convenient, but their business model usually includes selling ROCs, so again it is debatable whether the energy is above and beyond what would have been generated anyway.

Most other countries do not have a similar ROC system to the UK so purchasing green electricity is much less complicated and you can be more confident that your green electricity is fully 'additional'.

Selling excess electricity

It is the dream of many individuals and green businesses not only to generate enough electricity to cover their own needs, but also to sell any excess back to 'the grid' (the electricity distribution system). While this is a possibility, there are a number of issues you need to consider:

- Whether you will actually generate enough electricity to make a grid connection worthwhile as the bureaucracy can be a burden.
- The grid is set up for a small number of large generators, not a large number of small generators, therefore you may find that the distribution companies are less enthusiastic about accepting your electricity than you might hope.
- If the grid fails then, by UK law, all generating equipment must instantly cut out to stop the repairmen getting electrocuted. Therefore grid-connected renewables will not be available during blackouts.

If you do install renewable electricity generation in the UK, you have to decide whether or not to sell ROCs. If you do, you are helping to increase the overall renewables capacity in the country, but if you didn't do it, somebody else would have to. If you don't then you can claim the energy is truly sustainable as it is above and beyond that required by the Obligation.

Internationally, governments have been introducing 'Feed-In Tariffs' which guarantee a price for small generators connecting renewable energy to the grid. Such a tariff has been credited with expanding Germany's renewable energy to 12 per cent – far ahead of other countries. Other places with a Feed-In Tariff system include several Australian states, California, Spain and Israel, with plenty more in the pipeline.

Renewable technologies

Wind

Wind energy has been used for centuries, either through windmills to grind corn, or sailing ships as a form of transport. Modern wind turbines are simple, quiet and cheap, but problems arise because the wind is intermittent.

There has also been a backlash against wind from those who believe that turbines spoil the aesthetic value of landscapes. This conflict is exacerbated by the fact that areas of natural beauty are often some of the best sites to install wind turbines. Fortunately, it is rare for people to complain about turbines in an industrial environment.

Siting a wind turbine is a job for an expert. Turbines work most efficiently where the wind is free of turbulence caused by valleys, buildings and trees. Trendy micro-turbines sold for domestic purposes are useless in built up areas because the wind is so turbulent.

Wave and tidal energy

These methods take energy from the sea in different ways, but both are still under development. Energy from the bobbing effect of waves can be captured by floating booms or 'ducks'. The ducks move up and down with the surface of the water and the movement is converted into electricity. Unfortunately energy from waves is highly dependent on weather and sea conditions.

Tidal energy is more predictable and more powerful, but capturing it requires huge dams which could have a large impact on wildlife. As the tide comes in and out, water is forced through a turbine in the dam to generate electricity.

These energy sources are currently being exploited for the grid and are not usually considered for individual companies. If you do see this as an opportunity, then consult an expert.

Solar hot water

Solar hot water panels use the sun's energy to heat up water either to use for washing, or to pre-heat water before it goes into a standard boiler. They are usually fixed to roofs and are linked to an insulated tank. When the panel is warm enough, water is pumped around tubes to be heated and is then stored in the tank. The systems are very simple, effective and becoming quite cheap.

Solar photovoltaic

Solar photovoltaic (PV) panels convert the sun's energy into electricity directly. PV panels can be fixed to walls, roofs or even built into roof tiles. They are currently more expensive than other forms of electricity generation, but are becoming more popular for portable equipment and powering road signs.

Hydro-electric energy

Hydro-power is one of the oldest forms of energy generation. Waterwheels have been used for centuries to take energy from fast moving streams and rivers for grinding corn and powering looms. More recently, massive hydroelectric dams have been built to hold back rivers in reservoirs and use that energy to generate electricity. This is the biggest form of renewable electricity production in the world, but some people are concerned about the environmental problems of flooding valleys and disrupting river courses.

Micro-hydro systems generate smaller amounts of electricity from smaller sources of water.

Biofuels

Biofuels are derived from plants, the idea being that carbon dioxide emitted by their use will be absorbed by the following generation of plants.

- Biomass: usually refers to wood, but can include straw and even manure. This is becoming an important source of energy in the wood industry as there is always a plentiful supply of fuel;
- Biodiesel: this is made by reacting vegetable oils with methanol to produce fuel and glycerol. When it is warm it can be used as a direct substitute for diesel in many vehicles, when cold it must be used in a blend. Most bio-diesel sold in the UK is B5: 5 per cent biodiesel and 95 per cent fossil fuel;
- Bioethanol: this is made by distilling plant sugars to form industrial alcohol.

There is currently a raging controversy over biofuels as the land area that would be required to replace the world's fossil fuel consumption would be immense. This would compete with food production or require the clearance of the world's forests. The commentator George Monbiot claims that rain-forest clearance for the current palm oil production for biodiesel in Indonesia means that the biodiesel effectively releases ten times as much carbon dioxide as fossil fuels.[56]

In the UK, the National Farmers' Union estimates that there is enough set-aside land to produce 5 per cent of the country's fuel demand without causing any conflict with other land use.[57] Waste vegetable oil, whether used directly or converted to biodiesel, is regarded as a sustainable source of fuel, but supply is limited.

Geothermal energy

There are two methods of extracting heat from the ground:

1 Ground Source Heat Pumps (GSHP): these use a compressor to extract heat from either a coil buried just below the surface of the ground; or
2 'Hot rocks': if the geology of your location is suitable, you may be able to take heat from geothermally heated rock or hot water in aquifers.

Obviously you will need advice from geology experts and a large amount of money to extract heat from 'hot rocks', but GSHPs are becoming more popular.

The efficiency of a GSHP is expressed as a coefficient of performance (CoP) which is the ratio of energy out to energy in. A good GSHP will heat water to 35°C with a CoP of 4, but raising it to a higher temperature will reduce the CoP.

From an environmental point of view, you need to be careful with CoPs. Many people, particularly GSHP salesmen, will blithely say 'For each unit of energy you put in, you'll get four out', but they don't tell you that it is one unit of *electricity* in to get four units of *heat* out. Unless you are getting it from a renewable source, the carbon dioxide from producing electricity is at least twice the amount from producing the equivalent amount of gas. Roughly speaking, when heating a building, a good GSHP is only twice as good in terms of climate impacts as a decent gas boiler.

The hydrogen economy

One of the problems with many sources of energy is their intermittency: wind turbines don't work when the wind doesn't blow and solar systems require the sun to be shining. One solution is to use any excess electricity to convert water into hydrogen in an electrolyser. The hydrogen can then be stored and, when it is required, burnt in an internal combustion engine or converted back to water to produce electricity in a fuel cell. Hydrogen also allows renewable energy to be used as a fuel in mobile applications such as motor vehicles.

The big problem with the hydrogen economy is sourcing the hydrogen. Converting electrical energy to hydrogen and back again is only 25–40 per cent efficient, which is a waste of scarce renewable electricity.

Top ten tips for renewable energy

- Drive down your consumption of energy first.
- Purchasing green electricity is the easiest way of securing renewable energy; but…
- Ensure that the green electricity scheme is actually generating renewable energy to match what they are selling you.
- Wind is currently the most cost effective source of renewable energy.
- Tackle planning permission and community concerns on wind before investment.
- Micro wind turbines are useless in urban environments.

- Biofuels from crops are currently considered unsustainable.
- Biofuels from waste products are usually sustainable.
- Solar PV is an excellent option and prices are falling.
- If you are producing excess renewable electricity to sell to the 'grid', you must make a decision on whether to sell the ROCs and understand the implications of doing so.

Green Buildings

Buildings and the environment

Buildings have a huge impact on our environment. In the UK, the construction industry consumes 90 per cent of non-energy minerals extracted in the country each year. The production and transport of building materials account for 10 per cent of the country's energy consumption.[58] Once built, those buildings are responsible for 46 per cent of the country's annual CO_2 production.[59] Green building techniques can significantly reduce these impacts.

It follows that to go green, you must consider your business's buildings. Office buildings are particularly energy inefficient and those with air conditioning have a carbon footprint roughly twice those without.

In addition, in industrial nations, people spend approximately 80 per cent of their time indoors. Green buildings eliminate toxic materials and utilize fresh air and natural daylight, measures which improve our quality of life and have been shown to improve productivity at work.

To describe how to design green buildings would take a book in itself, and there are many available, so we can only give an overview here. Appendix 1 contains some recommended resources.

What is a green building?

Energy in use

The largest part of a standard building's ecological footprint is the energy it consumes while it is in use. It has been estimated that office buildings are responsible for up to one-sixth of the UK's carbon dioxide emissions (roughly equivalent to the energy intensive cement industry).

In domestic properties, heating is the major user of energy. In office accommodation, cooling tends to be the main culprit. This is because offices tend to be used during the day when the outdoor temperature is highest, the density of people is very high and the intensive use of IT equipment produces lots of waste heat.

The following measures will reduce this consumption:

- high levels of insulation (typically 300mm or equivalent);
- high performance windows (including low-e glass which traps heat inside the building when required);
- 'passive solar design' uses heat from the sun to heat and/or cool buildings;
- natural cooling systems can drag air into the building via cool basements and foundations;
- minimizing uncontrolled ventilation and installing mechanical ventilation with a heat exchanger to recover energy from the stale air being expelled;
- natural daylighting techniques which get daylight deep into the building (this will improve the welfare and productivity of your staff too);
- use of micro-renewables (see previous section) to produce low carbon electricity and heat.

Water

Techniques for reducing water consumption in kitchens and bathrooms were described in Chapter 4. More radical sustainable water management techniques include:

- rainwater harvesting: capturing water from roofs, filtering it, storing it and using it for non-potable uses like flushing toilets and washing machines in laundries;
- grey-water recycling: the reuse of water from sinks, showers etc for flushing toilets (although a number of studies have cast doubt on whether it is worthwhile as the soap in the water can 'go off');[60]
- water treatment: some buildings have on-site treatment systems for grey-water and even black-water (from toilets). These usually consist of biological treatment ponds. The most advanced type is a 'living machine' which uses a whole series of plants and microbes to treat water in a cascade of tanks;
- Sustainable Urban Drainage Systems (SUDS): these capture water and let it soak away rather than dumping it straight in a river which can cause flooding.

Note that many people say 'grey-water recycling' when they actually mean 'rain-water harvesting'. I don't know why they do, but they're wrong.

Building materials

We will be considering what makes a material 'green' in more detail later when we consider eco-design of products, but as a rule of thumb a green building should be built out of materials which:

- have a low embodied energy: embodied energy is the total energy required to extract raw materials, convert them into a useful form and get them on site. Low embodied energy materials include natural materials and recycled materials (i.e. 'Cyclic' in the ecological model);
- are non-toxic ('Safe' in the ecological model): toxic materials occur in paints, flooring, many fibreboards (MDF, chipboard, etc), PVC.

Other features

Other features that can be built into a green building include:

- ecological features: green roofs, bird/bat boxes, insect homes and climbing plants can all improve the biodiversity of your building;
- recycling provision: the building should be designed to accommodate recycling receptacles;
- transport links: you may want to site your building near to transport links so your staff can avoid having to travel by car;
- cycling provision: secure, covered cycle parking and showers will encourage staff to cycle to work;
- food production: some people build food-growing areas into their buildings.

Styles of green buildings

The different styles of green buildings are:

- greener conventional build: normal design, but using eco-friendly materials such as reclaimed brick, roof tiles and a high level of insulation;

- timber frame: sustainably sourced timber is a low impact material. High levels of insulation are also used along with other eco-friendly materials;
- passive solar design: these buildings are positioned and oriented to capture and store the sun's energy in a thermal mass (usually a thick concrete or brick wall), allowing heat to be released throughout the day and night;
- passive ventilation: buildings can be designed to use the wind to remove warm stale air, backed up with fans for days when the wind doesn't blow;
- Earthship: a particular style of passive solar building that uses scrap tyres full of rammed earth to provide the thermal mass – usually embedded into a hillside;
- straw bale construction: uses plastered straw bales for walls (although the resulting thick walls may lose too much space in the narrow site available and may have security implications).

The costs of all styles of buildings vary widely, therefore it is impossible to predict the cost of the building before a design is developed. Studies have shown no statistical difference between the costs of eco-friendly buildings and their conventional alternatives, not taking into consideration 'extras' such as micro-renewables and so on.[62]

How to specify a green building

In the UK, the Building Research Establishment (BRE) has a well-established method of evaluating the environmental performance of commercial buildings called BREEAM: the BRE Environmental Assessment Method. BREEAM is currently being formulated for international use in Europe and the Middle East. Other national schemes include the Leadership in Energy and Environmental Design (LEED) system in the US, the Passivhaus standard in Germany and GreenStar in Australia.

The BREEAM method awards points for the following categories:

- management: overall management policy, commissioning site management and procedural issues;
- energy use: operational energy and CO_2 issues;

- health and well-being: indoor and external issues affecting health and well-being;
- pollution: air and water pollution issues;
- transport: transport-related CO_2 and location-related factors;
- land use: greenfield and brownfield sites;
- ecology: ecological value conservation and enhancement of the site;
- materials: environmental implication of building materials, including life-cycle impacts;
- water: consumption and water efficiency.

Depending on the number of points the building receives, it will be given one of the following ratings:

- outstanding;
- excellent;
- very good;
- good;
- fair.

This makes it very easy to specify a green building. Simply appoint an architect with a good track record of eco-buildings and say 'I'd like this building to achieve BREEAM Excellent (or equivalent)'. The good track record part is important as there are numerous cases of passive solar heating/ventilation systems that do not work. Retro fitting air conditioning/heating systems is very expensive, so be warned!

Eco-renovation

Improving the environmental performance of an existing building is much trickier as you are stuck with the existing fabric and orientation. The following options are available:

- installing extra roof and floor insulation;
- cavity wall insulation where absent;
- external insulated cladding;

- internal wall insulation;
- upgrading windows and doors;
- window louvres to cut sunshine in summer.

Historic (pre-1919) buildings are particularly difficult to improve as they have been designed to allow the free flow of moisture so it is important to ensure moisture is not trapped and to avoid 'cold bridging' between the interior and the outside world which can cause condensation. For listed buildings, secondary glazing and roof/underfloor insulation are the best options.

Top ten tips for greening your building

- For new buildings, use a national green building rating such as BREEAM or LEED to specify performance.
- For eco-renovation, external cladding will make the biggest difference to energy performance.
- For pre-1919 buildings, ensure moisture is not trapped.
- For listed buildings, secondary glazing and roof/underfloor insulation are the best options.
- Reduce energy in use through insulation, passive solar gain/cooling and daylighting.
- Build in micro-renewables (but be careful with micro-wind in an urban setting).
- Choose low-embodied energy, non-toxic materials.
- Manage water through rainwater harvesting.
- Avoid grey-water recycling until technology improves.
- Build biodiversity into the building fabric and grounds.

Industrial Symbiosis

Beyond green procurement

In Chapter 4, we saw that green procurement was a simple, but powerful, way of improving your environmental performance. In this section we take that a step further by considering all and any businesses as potential suppliers or purchasers of material through the concept of 'Industrial Symbiosis' (IS). To explain the concept we'll take a quick trip to Denmark to see where it all began.

Kalundborg

Kalundborg is a sleepy little port of 20,000 people on the western coast of the Danish island of Zealand, famous for its remarkable five-towered red brick medieval church which looms over the cobbled streets and the red and yellow rendered houses of the old town. According to the tourist guides, that is pretty much all the town has to offer. But if you wind your way down to the water's edge, two monolithic blocks of a huge coal-fired power station dominate the view across the fjord. Just to the left and beyond the older block of this plant, the flickering flames of two flare stacks mark the location of an oil refinery. Further left again, but out of sight beyond the port's warehouses, is one of the world's biggest pharmaceutical plants. It is the story of these three industrial complexes, a number of smaller plants, the town itself and their unique symbiotic relationship that brings environmentalists on pilgrimages to Kalundborg from all over the world.

In the 1960s, the government decided to attract some big dirty industries to Kalundborg as it had become an unemployment blackspot. Planning regulations were relaxed and land was provided practically free of charge. The only problem was that there was no source of fresh water needed for all three plants except for Lake Tisso, over 25km away. So the plant managers worked together to cascade wastewater from one process to another, starting where it had to be cleanest and working its way down through the less fussy processes and recycling it wherever possible. The power station produced an excess of steam so it was piped the short distance to the other plants and then around the fjord to the town where it heats all the buildings. More companies turned up to take advantage of other opportunities: a plasterboard company which takes the gypsum from the power station's pollution control equipment to build into its products and a fish farm which uses (and cools) some of the warm wastewater. The pharma plant also produces a fertilizer product made from the process substrate. It is trademarked, but given away free to local farmers. If the company had to pay for disposal to landfill, the plant would go bust and 2700 local people would be unemployed.

On Earth Day 1989 a number of students were asked to study the environmental impact of the town's industries and they started to trace these connections. Using a pinboard and coloured string, they presented the findings to the companies' management teams. The industrialists hadn't realized just how integrated and interdependent their plants had become, so they set up a small institute to co-ordinate the relationships and started investing heavily in further synergies. Links have come and gone, but with the habit ingrained and the benefits proven, the infrastructure has simply been adapted to exploit new opportunities.

Of course this is not eco-nirvana. The power plant burns coal, the oil refinery provides fuel for planes, trains and automobiles, and fish farming is rarely seen as 'green'. But, given these processes are a fact of modern life, the environmental impacts have been minimized. Almost every last scrap of energy and water is used and waste arisings minimized. None of the individual links is unique to Kalundborg, in fact most are found somewhere in most industrialized nations with the notable exception of large-scale district heating. It is simply that nowhere else in the world can you find such a compact example of the benefits of IS.

What is IS?

Nature is not quite as red in tooth and claw as the more lurid TV nature programmes about predators would have us believe. All organisms live in symbiosis with others – a relationship where both parties benefit. For example, we could not survive without certain bacteria in our gut which help us digest food. They eat and we eat and both are happy.

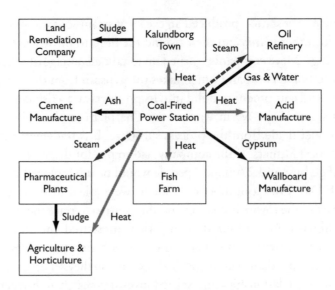

Figure 5.1 Simplified diagram of Industrial Symbiosis at Kalundborg[62]

As the name suggests, IS adopts this concept in industry. It has been defined as a process that: 'engages traditionally separate industries in a collective approach to competitive advantage involving physical exchange of materials, energy, water, and by-products'.[63]

In other words 'one company's waste becomes a raw material for another', but where waste includes anything that is being wasted. IS chimes neatly with my adage that 'waste is a verb, not a noun'.

Starting from scratch on Teesside

In February 2000 I was summoned to the University of Teesside for an interview for Centre Manager of the new Clean Environment Management Centre (CLEMANCE). I had spent the previous week swotting up on ideas for bringing sustainability to industry and had lighted on 'zero-waste clusters' from a book by Nelson Neremow[64] as an exciting concept that might set me apart from other candidates, which it obviously did as I got the job. It took me a further three years to get my ideas together and secure the necessary funding, but in January 2003 we were ready to start the Tees Valley Industrial Symbiosis Project (TVISP). It took another six months to recruit a project officer and a sufficient number of large companies to form a critical mass before we could publicly launch the project.

We worked the project around two streams of activity:

1 brainstorming: getting teams of representatives of the different businesses together, brainwashing them with the 'waste = resource' message and carrying out structured activities to generate innovative ideas using their combined brain power and experience;
2 data collecting: we visited companies to compile information on their inputs and outputs and manually matched compatible processes together.

The results were extraordinary. The ideas that were generated and then implemented managed to divert over 150,000 tonnes of waste per year from landfill going into the future and made the participants millions in profits. Examples included:

● potato waste from a food plant being composted and returned to farmland as a soil improver;
● 300,000 tomato plants being grown under glass using the waste heat from a fertilizer factory. Carbon dioxide from the factory is also introduced into the greenhouses to help ripen the fruit;
● offcuts from a plastics company being recycled into a range of products including plastic kerbstones with integrated drainage channels;
● one company providing another with excess steam and then taking back the condensate for recycling (this allowed an inefficient boiler to be decommissioned).

How to implement IS

Facilitation providers

By definition, you cannot go it alone on Industrial Symbiosis. You may have industrial contacts in your locality, or within your sector, and you could certainly approach them to discuss ideas for synergies. However you will find it more effective to use a third-party facilitator because:

- they will introduce you to a much wider range of potential partners from other sectors;
- they will have compiled a large database of opportunities to match with your inputs and outputs;
- facilitated brainstorming sessions, if done properly, can produce solutions that you wouldn't have thought of yourself.

At the time of writing, the UK is benefiting from facilitation from the National Industrial Symbiosis Programme (NISP). The NISP organization intends to expand overseas, but, if you don't have access to such a service, then you could always set one up through local trade bodies or business development agencies.

Top ten tips to implement IS

- Treat the word 'waste' as a verb, never a noun.
- Consider all 'wastes' including energy, water, logistics – any under-utilized resource.
- Don't forget to include your inputs as well as your outputs in the process.
- Think outside your sector.
- Use facilitation services where available.
- Engage a range of staff in the process including production engineers and business managers.
- As always, don't forget the business case. If both partners in a synergy won't benefit economically, it won't last.
- Don't minimize a 'waste stream' before you consider IS (we're going way beyond the waste hierarchy here).
- Don't forget about waste legislation. Even though green businesses don't believe in the noun 'waste', environmental regulators do and you will have to comply with your national waste management legislation.
- Try not to be too precious with information. A blanket insistence on Non-Disclosure Agreements (NDAs) can kill IS. They should only be used where genuine trade secrets could be at risk.

Eco-Design

Overview

It has been estimated that 80 per cent of the environmental impact of a product over its life cycle is determined before that product leaves the drawing board. This gives the designer a huge opportunity to design out environmental problems before they even exist. It is also the most cost effective way of going green as lines on a piece of paper or on a computer aided design system cost virtually nothing.

Function

An eco-product provides a function to the consumer with a minimum of impact on the environment, either through eco-efficiency or by following the ecological model. In order to meet the levels of innovation required for sustainability it is important to focus on the function and forget about the form of current products. Otherwise you will find yourself just tweaking an existing design.

Some example functions are:

- Do we need a car, or do we need a way of getting from A to B?
- Do we need a heater, or do we need a way of keeping warm?

We will be taking this idea to its logical extreme later with product service systems, but for the rest of this section we will assume that your product will have a physical form.

Whole life cycle thinking

Product life cycles

The classic 'cradle to grave' life cycle is shown in Figure 5.2 below.

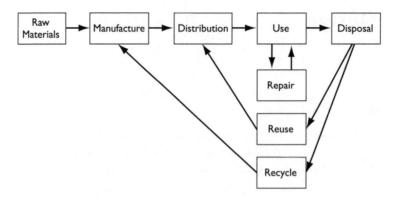

Figure 5.2 The product life cycle

It consists of the following stages:

- Raw materials extraction: getting non-renewable raw materials out of the Earth and refining them is a very dirty, energy intensive process. Production of renewable resources like wood and bio-plastics can also be environmentally damaging due to land use (and the resulting loss of natural habitat) and the requirement for chemicals and water in conventional agriculture and forestry.
- Manufacture: this single box represents an often complex supply chain consisting of many companies providing components to a final manufacturer.
- Distribution: moving products around the world and selling them in often energy inefficient shops and showrooms can be a significant part of the life cycle.
- Use: this is a tricky phase at it is usually outside the control of the designer, yet for energy-consuming products it is usually the most significant phase in the life cycle. The length of the use phase is usually down to fashion or economics rather than physical failure of the product. Expensive products are often repaired if they do last until failure, but cheaper products will normally go to disposal.
- Disposal: when the product finishes its use phase it can be landfilled, used to generate energy or reused/recycled. Some products are dispersed during

their use phase and do not have a formal 'disposal', e.g. perfumes, lubricants and solvents.
- Reuse: is when a whole product can be resold as it is or following refurbishment.
- Recycle: this is when the product is reduced to its component materials and fed back into the manufacturing chain either for a similar product or a completely different one.

Life Cycle Assessment

A few years ago, everyone was talking about Life Cycle Assessment (LCA). The technique requires the creation of an inventory containing every input and output relating to the product over its life cycle. In theory this inventory could be almost infinite, so in practice a 'system boundary' is drawn around the product which contains all the direct and/or major inputs and outputs, but omits minor and many indirect inputs and outputs. Once the inventory is complete, the environmental impacts of each input and output are calculated. Finally these are combined into a single 'score' using a subjective weighting of the importance of different types of environmental impact.

This final score is expressed as 'points per functional unit' where the functional unit is a measure of the use of the product. This means that different products providing the same service can be compared, for example:

- For freight the functional unit is usually 'tonne kilometres' – so the result of the LCA is the impact of moving one tonne of cargo one kilometre whether it is moved by ship, road or air.
- Likewise 'passenger kilometres' is the standard functional unit for personal and public transport.

Functional units measure utility, so LCA gives an eco-efficiency measure (see Chapter 2 for details).

There are a number of problems with LCA:

- time and effort: compiling an inventory for even the simplest product is a substantial undertaking. One tele-communications company told me they budget for £10,000 *per component* and their products have hundreds of components;

- WYGIWYN: What You Get Is What You Need – the results of most comparative LCAs favour the sponsor's product over their rivals';
- the results of many LCAs are highly dependent on a small number of assumptions, many relating to the life cycle which are hard to test or indeed control;
- with a bit of experience, most results can be predicted beforehand.

Having worked on LCAs, I have decided that:

> Life is too short for Life Cycle Assessment.

On the other hand, generic LCA data on materials can be very useful and is available commercially.

Eco-design methodology

The eco-design approach adopted in this book is the same as proposed in Chapter 2, namely:

- go Solar, Cyclic, Safe and, where not,
- be efficient with a target of factor 10.

These are translated into a number of elements:

- materials selection matrix;
- energy ratings;
- eco-efficiency measures;
- design for disassembly.

I propose that all of these elements are applied using 80:20 type thinking. In other words, if you can't easily distinguish between two options, then there is no point in worrying about it.

Materials selection matrix

We saw in Chapter 2 that we should be using materials that can be defined as a biological or technical nutrient, in other words they should be safe *and* cyclic. Table 5.1 below shows a rating scheme for each attribute. Using the two resulting ratings, the desirability of a material can be determined from the Materials Selection Matrix (see Figure 5.3).

These ratings should be interpreted as follows:

- High (H): a true technical/biological nutrient. Use as much as you like within the limits of a sustainable supply.
- Medium (M) while not a true nutrient, it is preferable over many alternatives. Use where there is no better alternative and then as efficiently as possible (e.g. factor 10).
- Low (L): only to be used where there is no alternative, and then as efficiently as possible. In addition measures should be put in place where possible to protect humans and the environment from such substances (these are effectively Grey List substances – see 'Greening your Supply Chain' in Chapter 4).
- eXclude (X): clearly not a nutrient – do not use at all. This is equivalent to a 'black list' material (see Chapter 4).

Table 5.1 *Material attribute ratings*

	Safe	Cyclic
High	Little or no risk. Can you eat it?	Material is recycled or biologically sourced *and* recyclable or biodegradable.
Medium	Low to moderate risk.	Either recycled or recyclable but not both.
Low	High risk. Mutagens, carcinogens, endocrine disrupters etc	Material is not recycled or recyclable, and is non-biodegradable.

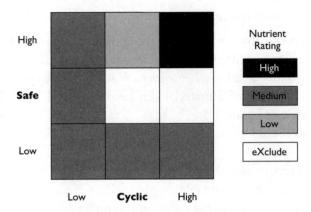

Figure 5.3 Materials selection matrix

In summary: strive to only use highly rated materials. Where this is impossible, use medium and/or low rated materials efficiently (efficiency measures are described below). 'X' rated materials should never be used in a green product.

Energy use

Ideally, all energy throughout the product lifecycle should come from 'solar' or 'renewable' resources, for example:

- direct solar power in the form of heat or electricity;
- biomass (wood, hemp, anaerobic digestion of waste etc) *from a sustainable supply*;
- muscle power (e.g. clockwork radio, bicycle);
- wind;
- wave or tidal energy.

For products using mains electricity in their use phase (e.g. vehicles, electrical goods), it is possible that this mains electricity could come from a solar source (e.g. biofuels, 'green' mains electricity). However, such products should be designed to be highly energy efficient because:

- in the short term the vast majority of energy will come from non-renewable sources as users generally have to 'opt-in' to renewable energy schemes;
- as we have seen before, renewable energy technology is unlikely to be capable of supplying current levels of energy demand in the medium term.

In summary, if you can ensure that your energy sources are 100 per cent solar then use as much energy as you like within the limits of supply. If not, be efficient. Some efficiency measures are described in the following section.

The rating system is as follows:

- High (H): directly solar powered: use as much energy as can be collected.
- Medium (M): could be indirectly solar powered (e.g. mains electricity) – be as efficient as possible.
- Excluded (X): definitely not solar powered (e.g. a coal-fired stove) – do not use – seek new source of energy.

It is recommended that, where in doubt, embodied energy in components be rated as 'medium', as tracing the type of energy used in material extraction and component manufacture would turn the framework into an LCA-type exercise.

Efficiency measures

Any material or energy rated 'medium' or 'low' should be used efficiently. The sections below describe some common ways of doing this.

Materials efficiency

The following efficiency methods can be used:

- lightweighting: reducing the weight of components. This is cumulative – reducing the weight of one component can reduce the amount of material required to support it;

- replacing material with air, e.g. inflatable packaging, furniture etc;
- replacing material with information, e.g. a better control system in a domestic washing machine can lead to reduced detergent and water use.

Energy efficiency

The following energy efficiency methods can be used:

- lightweighting can also improve the energy efficiency of products with moving parts;
- increasing thermal insulation;
- reducing electrical resistance;
- reducing mechanical friction;
- replacing energy with information, e.g. an engine management system in a car can lead to reduced fuel consumption.

Utility extension

One of the easiest ways of (apparently) improving the eco-efficiency of a product is to improve the amount of utility extracted from it. This can be done in two ways:

1   extending the physical life cycle of the product;
2   making the product multi-functional.

The idea of both approaches is that the extra utility will avoid the need to use other products. Unfortunately the reality is not so simple.

The lifespan of a product is difficult to predict as it is often a function of fashion or economic value rather than its physical lifespan. Manufacturers of mobile phones often claim that their products will last 10 years, but in practice most phones are upgraded within a year as users desire the latest model. This goes for products as large as ships, which are scrapped when their economic value drops below their scrap value, rather than when they are in an irreparable state. This is an easy 'false eco-efficiency' trap to fall into.

Making the product multifunctional puts the emphasis on the consumer to change their consumption patterns to match the new product. Last year I bought a mobile phone that will play MP3s and take photographs, but I already had an MP3 player and a digital camera (both of which carry out their functions better than the mobile). So I have plenty of functionality, but no environmental improvement.

My advice is to steer clear of utility extension as an eco-design strategy, unless you have control over the product in its use phase. We will be discussing this in 'Product Service Systems' later.

Design for disassembly

If we want to be true to the 'Cyclic' principle of 'Solar, Cyclic, Safe', we need to be able to recover materials from products after use. The following methods can make disassembly of products easier:

- use fewer materials, e.g. William McDonough and Michael Braungart's book *Cradle to Cradle* is made out of a single polymer so it can simply be melted down and recycled;
- move from composite materials to mono-materials which are easy to recycle;
- minimize the number of different types of materials;
- modularize design to facilitate reuse of subsystems;
- label materials for easy identification and sorting;
- minimize the number of fastenings;
- use fastenings that are easy to open (e.g. snap fastenings over screws, avoid glues etc);
- develop new sorting technologies: e.g. the use of 'smart plastics' to allow products to self-dissemble when heated to a certain temperature. The plastics can be 'programmed' to deform to lose clips and screw threads.

Advanced eco-design techniques

There are a number of advanced design methods that have shown good results for eco-design. These are generally too complex to describe here, but the sections below will give you a flavour.

Bio-mimicry

Janine Benyus is the main cheerleader for the environmental benefits of borrowing design ideas from the natural world around us.[65] Her argument is that nature optimizes products over hundreds of millions of years and has produced many miracles such as:

- spider's silk: a waterproof fibre, five times stronger than steel, yet produced at room temperature and pressure;
- the leaf: which converts sunlight to fuel much more efficiently than the best photovoltaic cell;
- abalone shell: this is twice as tough as any manmade ceramic.

TRIZ

TRIZ is the Russian System of Inventive Problem Solving.[66] The underlying idea of TRIZ is that innovation is predictable. It provides a set of generic innovative methods that have been distilled from the painstaking analysis of millions of patents. The 'ideal solution' that TRIZ aims to achieve is the one that delivers the service required without consuming any resources – this has obvious environmental benefits.

The TRIZ process involves modelling the problem using a variety of tools, then applying the generic innovation principles to each part of the model in a structured way until a solution 'fits'. It works in much the same way as the keywords in Hazard and Operability (HAZOP) analysis. If you do a lot of product development then TRIZ is definitely worth a look.

Top ten tips for eco-design

- Focus on the function.
- Consider the whole life cycle; but,
- Life's too short for LCA.
- Go Solar, Cyclic, Safe and, where not,
- Be efficient with a target of factor 10.
- Design out all toxic materials.

- Design for easy disassembly.
- Design out inefficient use of the product (e.g. standby switches).
- Avoid utility extension as a strategy.
- Design your product with marketing in mind (see 'Marketing green products and services' in Chapter 3).

Product Service Systems

What is a product service system?

The idea of a product service system is to replace a product's physical form with an intangible service instead. This takes the eco-design principle of focusing on the function of the product to the ultimate degree. A car manufacturer may believe that they make cars, but fundamentally they provide a method of getting from A to B. By thinking about the service provided, rather than a tangible product, a more efficient transport service could be provided instead, for example a car club.

The traditional making and selling product industrial model means that profit is related to the amount of physical product shifted. A product service system breaks this link as profit is only related to the amount of service provided – material is simply an additional cost. Figure 5.4 below shows how this works. There are two types of product service system:

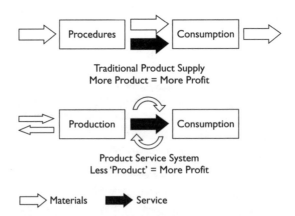

Figure 5.4 Product service system versus a traditional product

1 where the physical 'product' is owned by the service provider and lent to the user before being taken back (e.g. a car club) as denoted by the curved arrows;
2 where the service has been stripped of physical manifestation altogether (e.g. downloading MP3s and eBooks).

Examples

There are many examples of product service systems in everyday life:

- Apple's iTunes sells music in a digital format without it ever becoming a tangible object like a vinyl record or a CD (note that if you then burn the music yourself on to a blank CD the environmental benefits evaporate)
- Many cable TV companies now offer 'movies on demand' – the entertainment is provided without becoming a physical product such as a video tape or DVD
- Any library offering books, CDs or DVDs is effectively providing its customers with the service they require (entertainment or information) without them having to purchase a physical artefact
- Interface Inc. is a carpet manufacturer turned floor covering service provider. Interface will provide office carpet tiles on a lease basis, replacing and remanufacturing or recycling worn tiles each year
- Bill Ford, Chairman of the Ford Motor Company, sees a future where car companies provide transport services rather than selling cars. Given the prestige value of cars and how attached their owners can become, this will be quite a challenge
- In the US, energy companies have found it cheaper to save energy by providing their customers with insulation than by generating more electricity. This is known as Demand Side Management: defining the end-use service and working out the least-cost method of supplying it
- Chemical management services: a number of companies will not only provide you with a chemical, e.g. a solvent, but will provide the equipment and take away the spent chemical for recycling
- Real nappy services: soiled nappies are collected from households and replaced with freshly laundered nappies.

Service design

Service design is an art in itself – as complex if not more so than designing a product. However it is usually possible continually to improve the service without expensive product withdrawals and relaunches.

Benefits and problems

The big benefit of a product service system is that it disconnects the link between consumption and resource use. Other benefits include:

- the service can be continually updated, more cheaply than improving a physical product;
- the provider keeps control over the product life cycle, particularly when the physical product is disposed of;
- the continuing relationship with the customer means that the provider can ensure that the product is used most effectively;
- an income stream is guaranteed into the future.

However there are a number of drawbacks including:

- culture change in customers: persuading a customer to pay for a service when they are used to a physical product can be difficult;
- fulfilling all the functions that a consumer desires, e.g. car ownership, provides services such as prestige, comfort, fun and perceived safety. This may make it difficult to sell a car club service to consumers who value these qualities;
- financing: you may have to invest upfront on the physical side of the service (e.g. buying cars for a car club), but income from those services will be spread over a longer period;
- risk: any upfront cost makes this a higher risk approach.

Top five tips for product service systems

- Strip the function of your product/service as far back as you can to identify the core need it satisfies.
- Market test like mad before making a big investment.
- Market the product/service on the positive cost/performance/ convenience benefits.
- Design the service properly: get service design experts in if necessary.
- Understand that you will have to re-orient most of your business functions to support the new business model.

Exploiting Synergies

Joined up thinking

The previous sections have described the most powerful environmental strategies for industry. The next level is to do some joined up thinking and combine some of these to get breakthrough solutions. For example:

- Combined eco-design and IS leads to 'designer offal', designing the product so the production process by-products have a better economic value. I have worked with a steel company who had changed their product slightly to give its main by-product, blast furnace slag, better properties for use as a substitute for aggregate in road building.
- Combined eco-design and product service system will ensure that the overall environmental impact of the system is minimized. Xerox design their photocopiers for a long life, making components robust and easily upgradeable.
- Combined IS and product service systems: one solution developed by the TVISP had one company providing solvent services to another as the best way of reusing waste solvents.

This is where true creativity can be used to develop groundbreaking solutions and finding synergies is extremely rewarding.

Identifying synergies

The backcasting approach described in Chapter 3 not only helps identify and resolve any conflicts between the changes describe in this section, it can also be used to identify potential synergies, such as those listed above.

You will find that members of your team may start to baulk at such complexity. I recommend that you consider the following:

- training staff in the techniques described in this book so they become comfortable with formulating the solutions;
- using an external facilitator in backcasting and other planning meetings to ask the 'why can't you also…?' questions;
- ensure that you rigorously challenge solutions in the later post-creativity stages to ensure that risk is not spiralling out of control. After all, you are running a business.

Conclusion

Final Thoughts

Hold on a mo...

Isn't all this environmental stuff meant to be really dull? I hope you now agree that this stuff is far too important and exciting to be dumped on the Quality/Health and Safety/Whatever manager. To build a truly green business, you need to carry out a root and branch re-evaluation of your organization. This is going to take leadership, vision and business acumen.

Of course, if you are lucky/brave enough to be starting your business from scratch, then you can avoid most of the barriers that face managers of existing organizations.

The tools in this book

Just to recap, this book has provided you with the Three Secrets of a Green Business:

1 understand the business case: be proactive, grasp the opportunity, but don't forget you are a business, not a charity;
2 follow the ecological model of sustainability, or where you can't, be eco-efficient by a factor 10;
3 take huge leaps and small steps.

Chapters 3, 4 and 5 of this book then explained how to put these into action:

- Chapter 3, Preparing To Go Green, explained how to manage change, how to engage staff and stakeholders, how to develop your strategy, how to communicate green marketing messages and how to use an environmental management system (EMS) to your best advantage.
- Chapter 4, Small Steps, detailed the small steps you will need to take to continually improve the environmental and economic performance of your business: waste minimization, energy efficiency, water conservation, green procurement, green travel planning and carbon offsetting.

- Chapter 5, Huge Leaps, described the most powerful techniques for a green business: cleaner production, renewable energy, eco-building, Industrial Symbiosis (IS), eco-design and product service systems.

It is not too much of a stretch to say that if you integrate all of these techniques that are applicable to your business, then you will have a truly green business.

Need help?

I have tried to structure this book to give you the knowledge and tools you need to create a genuinely green business. However, the scope of the skills required is immense and you might find you need some external help. The following areas are where you might want to buy in expertise:

- training and awareness;
- facilitation of backcasting sessions;
- developing an EMS;
- auditing/measuring your baseline;
- green travel planning;
- product design;
- service design;
- cleaner production: sector experts;
- PR, marketing and communications;
- architectural design, construction and building services engineers.

If you do contract external help, I advise the following:

- Be clear about the outcomes, but, within reason, leave the methodology to the consultant. Unless they are very poor at their job, they will have a better idea of how to deliver than you will. Focus on the 'what'.
- Don't insist on hourly/daily rates. This encourages consultants to produce long reports, type slowly, insist on loads of meetings, or indeed fib. It is much better for client and consultant to agree a fixed fee.

- Use government subsidized schemes where they are appropriate (i.e. small steps), but they can be too restrictive for more complex problems (i.e. huge leaps).

Appendix 1 describes some of the types of help available in the UK.

So why don't you get started?

Appendix 1: Sources of Help

Support Schemes

Subsidized help versus consultancy

Over the last decade, the UK government has set up a myriad of business support schemes, for example Envirowise and the Carbon Trust. While this is admirable there are a number of advantages to getting paid help.

Advantages of government help

- lower/no cost;
- quality assurance of providers: all the government schemes have rigorous selection criteria;
- easy to find: the government schemes are very well promoted.

Advantages of consultancy

- flexibility: an independent consultant will only be working for you and you can engage them to do exactly what you want rather than working through a preordained programme;
- scope: the government schemes tend to focus on small steps and are unlikely to deliver huge leaps.

UK government schemes

At the time of writing UK companies may be eligible for support from the following:

- Envirowise: operates a helpline for queries, provides a large number of free publications, www.envirowise.gov.uk, last accessed 7 September 2009. Unfortunately FastTrack waste minimization visits have been discontinued.
- The Carbon Trust: a large number of publications, free consultancy for larger energy users, www.carbontrust.co.uk, last accessed 7 September 2009.

- Waste Resources Action Programme (WRAP): funds research work leading to improved markets for recycled materials, www.wrap.org.uk, last accessed 7 September 2009.
- National Industrial Symbiosis Programme (NISP): provides industrial symbiosis facilitation services, www.nisp.org.uk, last accessed 7 September 2009.
- Low Carbon Buildings Programme: provides subsidies for renewable energy technologies for domestic users, public sector and charities, www.lowcarbonbuildings.org.uk, last accessed 7 September 2009.
- And many, many more. Contact your local or regional authority for more.

Useful Books and Websites

Introduction

The following are my recommendations for further reading. All links are live at the time of writing.

General resources

- von Weizsäcker, E., Lovins A. B. and Lovins, L. H. (1997) *Factor Four: Doubling Wealth, Halving Resource Use*, Earthscan, London;
- Hawkens, P., Lovins, A. B. and Lovins, L. H. (2000) *Natural Capitalism*, Earthscan, London or see www.natcap.org;
- Jackson, T. (1996) *Material Concerns: Pollution, Profit and Quality of Life*, Routledge, London;
- Datchefski, E. (2001) *The Total Beauty of Sustainable Products*, Rotovision, Crans-Près-Céligny
- Benyus, J. M. (1996) *Biomimicry*, Perennial, New York, or see www.biomimicry.org;
- McDonough, W. and Braungart, M. (2002) *Cradle to Cradle: Remaking the Way We Make Things*, North Point Press, New York;
- Senge, P., Kruschwitz, N., Laur, J. and Schley, S. (2008) *The Necessary Revolution*, Nicholas Brearley, London;
- 'The Low Carbon Agenda': my own monthly newsletter, www.terrainfirma.co.uk/resources.html;
- NetRegs is the UK's 'plain English' guide to environmental legislation, www.netregs.gov.uk;
- The Sustainability Forum is an online forum for all in this field: www.sustainabilityforum.com.

Change management

- Walker, P. (2006) *Change Management for Sustainable Development*, IEMA, Lincoln – www.iema.net/shop;
- Senge, P., Kruschwitz, N., Laur, J. and Schley, S. (2008) *The Necessary Revolution*, Nicholas Brearley, London

Environmental management systems

- Edwards, A. J. (2003) *ISO 14001 Environmental Certification Step by Step*, Butterworth-Heinemann, Oxford;
- British Standards Institute, available at www.bsi-global.com.

Green marketing

- Grant, J. (2007) *The Green Marketing Manifesto*, John Wiley & Sons, Chichester.

Pollution incident prevention

- Environment Agency Guide to the basic principles of pollution incident prevention, available at http://publications.environment-agency.gov.uk/pdf/PMHO0501BFOX-e-e.pdf;
- NetRegs is the UK's 'plain English' guide to environmental legislation, available at www.netregs.gov.uk;
- Taylor, B. J., Crawley, F. and Preston, M. L. (2008) *HAZOP: Guide to Best Practice*, Institute of Chemical Engineers, London;
- McDermott, R. E., Mikulak, R. J. and Beauregard, M. R. (1996) *Basics of FMEA*, Productivity Press, New York.

Waste minimization

- The Envirowise website (available at www.envirowise.gov.uk) has a large number of waste minimization case studies in a wide range of sectors.

Energy efficiency

- The Carbon Trust website (available at www.carbontrust.co.uk) has a whole range of useful information on saving energy in the workplace.

Water conservation

- The Envirowise website (available at www.envirowise.gov.uk) has a large number of water conservation case studies in a wide range of sectors.

Green transport planning

- Green Transport Plans, Department of Transport, available at www.dft.gov.uk/pgr/sustainable/travelplans;
- Energy Savings Trust Fleet Project, available at www.energysavingtrust.org.uk/fleet.

Cleaner production

- Jackson, T. (1996) *Material Concerns: Pollution, Profit and Quality of Life*, Routledge, London;
- The Envirowise website (available at www.envirowise.gov.uk) has a large number of cleaner production case studies in a wide range of sectors.

Renewable energy

- The Energy Savings Trust, available at www.energysavingtrust.org.uk.

Green building

- Hall, K. (2006) *The Green Building Bible*, Green Building Press, Llandysul;
- Building Research Establishment Environmental Assessment Method (BREEAM) Scheme, available at www.breeam.org;
- Green Building Forum, available at www.greenbuildingforum.co.uk.

Industrial Symbiosis

- National Industrial Symbiosis Programme (NISP) for case studies, available at www.nisp.org.uk;
- The Kalundborg Symbiosis Institute oversees the synergies between companies in Kalundborg, Denmark, available at www.symbiosis.dk;
- The International Society for Industrial Ecology (ISIE) is the academic body that oversees IS research, available at www.is4ie.org.

Eco-design

- Datchefski, E. (2001) *The Total Beauty of Sustainable Products*, Rotovision, Crans-Près-Céligny;
- Benyus, J. M. (1966) *Biomimicry*, Perennial, New York, or see www.biomimicry.org
- McDonough, W., and Braungart, M. (2002) *Cradle to Cradle: Remaking the Way We Make Things*, North Point Press, New York;
- Fuad-Luke, A. (2002) *The Eco-design Handbook*, Thames & Hudson, London.

Product service systems

- Hawkens, P., Lovins, A. B. and Lovins, L. H. (2002) *Natural Capitalism*, Earthscan, London, or see www.natcap.org

Appendix 2: Checklists

Small Steps

- ❏ pollution incident prevention;

- ❏ waste minimization and recycling;

- ❏ energy efficiency;

- ❏ water conservation;

- ❏ green procurement;

- ❏ green transport planning;

- ❏ carbon offsetting.

Huge Leaps

- ❏ cleaner production;

- ❏ renewable energy;

- ❏ Industrial Symbiosis;

- ❏ eco-building;

- ❏ eco-design;

- ❏ product service systems.

Top Tips: Culture Change

❑ Make a commitment through an environmental policy.

❑ Keep the policy to one page of A4.

❑ Go out of your way to 'walk the walk', even when the going gets tough.

❑ Engage your staff and make them part of the solution.

❑ Make an appropriate financial commitment.

❑ Set up staff committees to develop 'small steps'.

❑ Set up action teams for 'huge leaps'.

❑ Implement simple incentive schemes, but with great care.

❑ Provide feedback to all staff.

❑ Match your tone to the company culture.

Top Tips: Environmental Management Systems

☐ Get proper commitment from the top.

☐ Make sure everyone understands the commitment to continual improvement.

☐ Make sure the system is properly resourced.

☐ If you employ consultants, make sure they deliver an elegant, easy-to-use system.

☐ Use an EMS as a framework for small steps and to monitor the results of huge leaps.

☐ Get the system running smoothly before going for certification.

☐ Engage as many staff as possible in the process.

☐ Most service sector organizations base their system on ISO 14001, but many don't go for accreditation.

☐ Consider BS 8555 to phase in an EMS over a period of time (see p46).

☐ Integrate the process into quality and health and safety management systems where possible to save resources.

Top Tips: Green Marketing

❏ Don't forget the hyenas: they will jump on any fault.

❏ For consumer products, resist the temptation to go overboard on the 'green look'.

❏ For business services and products, focus on business benefits such as reduced costs.

❏ Design your product and/or service so they can compete on performance and/or price.

❏ Market the product in an assured manner – if you are wishy-washy then that will reflect on your product.

❏ If you are targeting a green niche then do play the green card more strongly.

❏ Use eco-labels or other recognized accreditation wherever possible.

❏ Avoid spurious claims or overstating your case.

❏ Avoid vagueness.

❏ Publish data to back up your claims, e.g. on your website.

Top Tips: Pollution Prevention

❑ Carry out risk assessments.

❑ Remove hazardous materials from your inventory wherever possible.

❑ Design your process to minimize the opportunities for an incident happening.

❑ Keep well-maintained spill kits near any store of hazardous material.

❑ Train staff to deal with all spills immediately.

❑ Map, understand and colour code your on-site drainage.

❑ Check bunds are water tight; people have a nasty habit of knocking a hole in the side to let rainwater out.

❑ Check that nozzles and pipes do not reach over the sides of bunds at ground level.

❑ Walk your site regularly and have a zero tolerance for unsafe working practices and bodges.

❑ Make being responsible for a pollution incident through negligence a disciplinary offence.

Top Tips: Waste Minimization

Top ten tips for offices

☐ Set all printers and photocopiers to double-sided printing as a default.

☐ Provide all internal documentation in electronic format and use electronic media for invitations and registration for meetings, conferences etc.

☐ Place a paper recycling bin in every office and a general waste bin at the end of each corridor.

☐ Use overhead projectors and PowerPoint at meetings rather than handouts. Make the presentations available on-line instead.

☐ Plan food for meetings carefully and let other staff know when there might be leftovers.

☐ Keep a tight control on ordering stationery.

☐ Encourage staff to reuse folders, box files etc.

☐ Use multi-use envelopes for internal mail and restrict the supply so staff have to re-use them.

☐ Discourage epic reports.

☐ Avoid disposable crockery and cutlery.

Top ten tips for factories

☐ Engage all staff in the process – they will know where waste occurs better than you.

☐ Provide separate, distinctive bins or skips for recyclable materials.

☐ Pay careful attention to packaging and dispatch areas.

☐ Ask suppliers to minimize or to take back packaging, or at least to design it for easy recycling.

☐ Reuse packaging internally, e.g. pallets and cartons.

☐ Carry out maintenance checks on machinery on a regular basis.

☐ Keep a tight control on stores to avoid casual overuse of materials.

☐ Design your product to minimize waste.

☐ Make your packaging appropriate to protect your product – not too much or too little.

☐ Avoid over-ordering raw materials, lubricants, spares, etc.

Top Tips: Energy Efficiency

Top ten tips for offices

❑ Run a 'Switch it off' campaign.

❑ Provide feedback to your staff on energy consumption.

❑ Purchase EnergyStar compliant or equivalent office equipment.

❑ Upgrade all lighting to the most energy efficient models.

❑ Downgrade the level of lighting in non-critical areas.

❑ Install automatic lighting controls, particularly for windowless rooms.

❑ Set heating controls to the optimum temperature and make sure they remain there.

❑ Make sure your heating tracks the temperature outside in the spring and autumn.

❑ Install a tea urn rather than individual kettles.

❑ Unplug laptops and other portable equipment to stop batteries discharging.

Top ten tips for factories

❏ Launch a 'Switch it off' campaign – calculate how much your business is losing and display this with the message.

❏ Install curtains at all entrances and exits.

❏ Zone heating and lighting systems so they can be adjusted to shift patterns.

❏ Check your air compressor is installed correctly and takes its air intake from outside.

❏ Check for compressed air leaks. Walk around in downtime to hear leaks or invest in an ultrasonic detector.

❏ Identify opportunities for waste heat recovery, such as capturing hot air and/or hot water from compressors.

❏ Make sure cold room and refrigerator doors are alarmed so staff are alerted if they are left open.

❏ Implement an upgrade plan for motors, and always buy the most efficient mode.

❏ Install variable speed drives where appropriate.

❏ Make sure all hot water pipes and fittings are adequately lagged.

Top Tips: Water Conservation

Top five tips for offices

❏ Installing percussion (push) taps on all wash hand basins can cut water use by 50 per cent.

❏ Install waterless urinals and low flush toilets.

❏ Purchase water conserving dishwashing machines and other such goods.

❏ Make sure there is a system for fixing leaks as soon as they are reported.

❏ Consider rainwater harvesting for toilets.

Top five tips for factories

❏ Fix all leaks and overflows immediately.

❏ Install trigger nozzles on all hoses.

❏ Use a brush to sweep up slurries rather than using a hose.

❏ Use rainwater for low grade water use like yard cleaning.

❏ Cascade water from high purity uses to lower grade uses (e.g. using 'last rinse' water for the next 'first wash').

Top Tips: Green Procurement

☐ Buy less stuff, or buy better stuff.

☐ Eliminate what you don't need.

☐ Order quantities to tightly match your needs.

☐ Minimize the use of lengthy supplier questionnaires.

☐ Buy services rather than products where possible.

☐ Analyse options using the Solar, Cyclic, Safe efficient criteria.

☐ Work with your suppliers to match specification to your needs.

☐ Work with your suppliers to optimize packaging.

☐ Research suppliers' backgrounds to ensure you will not get blamed for their sins.

☐ Draw up black and grey lists to screen out toxic materials.

Top Tips: Transport

❑ Produce a green travel plan.

❑ Rationalize parking to encourage other forms of commuting.

❑ Provide bicycle racks, lockers and showers.

❑ Negotiate with public transport providers to optimize routes.

❑ Hire or purchase efficient vehicles.

❑ Use alternative (low carbon) fuels.

❑ Train staff on fuel efficient driving techniques.

❑ Discourage unnecessary travel through teleconferencing and back-loading of freight.

❑ Eliminate unauthorized travel.

❑ Encourage telecommuting.

Top Tips: Cleaner Production

❑ Forget 'how you've always done things'.

❑ Adopt an 'invest to save' culture.

❑ Plot your production process and engage your staff on potential solutions.

❑ Use 'The Toddler Test' – for each part of the process keep asking 'Why?' to determine whether an element is needed or being carried out in the best way.

❑ Consult your sector organizations and publications to keep abreast of best practice.

❑ Look at other sectors and cross fertilize ideas.

❑ Engage with universities and other research bodies.

❑ Use the resources listed in Appendix 1 to identify possible solutions.

❑ Carry out rigorous risk analyses of new technologies.

❑ Watch out for snake oil salesmen.

Top Tips: Renewable Energy

❏ Drive down your consumption of energy first.

❏ Purchasing green electricity is the easiest way of securing renewable energy; but…

❏ Ensure that the green electricity scheme is actually generating renewable energy to match what they are selling you.

❏ Wind is currently the most cost effective source of renewable energy.

❏ Tackle planning permission and community concerns on wind before investment.

❏ Micro wind turbines are useless in urban environments.

❏ Biofuels from crops are currently considered unsustainable.

❏ Biofuels from waste products are usually sustainable.

❏ Solar PV is an excellent option and prices are falling.

❏ If you are producing excess renewable electricity to sell to the 'grid', you must make a decision on whether to sell the Renewable Obligation Certificates (ROCs) and understand the implications of doing so.

Top Tips: Greening Buildings

❏ For new buildings, use the BREEAM or an equivalent rating scheme to specify performance.

❏ For eco-renovation, external cladding is generally the best option.

❏ For pre-1919 buildings, ensure moisture is not trapped.

❏ For listed buildings, secondary glazing and roof/underfloor insulation are the best options.

❏ Reduce energy in use through insulation, passive solar gain/cooling and daylighting.

❏ Build in micro-renewables.

❏ Choose low-embodied energy, non-toxic materials.

❏ Manage water through rainwater harvesting.

❏ Avoid grey-water recycling until technology improves.

❏ Build biodiversity into the building fabric and grounds.

Top Tips: Industrial Symbiosis

❏ Treat the word 'waste' as a verb, never as a noun.

❏ Consider all 'wastes' including energy, water, logistics – any under-utilized resource.

❏ Don't forget to include your inputs as well as your outputs in the process.

❏ Think outside your sector.

❏ Use facilitation services where available.

❏ Engage a range of staff in the process including production engineers and business managers.

❏ As always, don't forget the business case. If both partners in a synergy won't benefit economically, it won't last.

❏ Don't minimize a 'waste stream' before you consider IS.

❏ Don't forget about waste legislation.

❏ Try not to be too precious with information.

Top Tips: Eco-Design

❑ Focus on the function.

❑ Consider the whole life cycle; but,

❑ Life's too short for Life Cycle Assessment (LCA).

❑ Go Solar, Cyclic, Safe and, where not,

❑ Be efficient with a target of factor 10.

❑ Design out all toxic materials.

❑ Design for easy disassembly.

❑ Design out inefficient use of the product (e.g. standby switches).

❑ Avoid utility extension as a strategy.

❑ Design your product with marketing in mind (see 'marketing green products and services' in Chapter 3).

Top Tips: Product Service Systems

❑ Strip the function of your product/service as far back as you can.

❑ Market test like mad before making a big investment.

❑ Market the product/service on the positive cost/performance/convenience benefits.

❑ Design the service properly: get service design experts in if necessary.

❑ Understand that you will have to re-orient most of your business functions to support the new business model.

Appendix 3: Brainstorming Tool

Brainstorming Tool

In order to support brainstorming exercises, I have developed the Terra Infirma brainstorming tool (see Figure A3.1). It is based on a fishbone diagram and is designed to ensure that brainstorming exercises cover all the causes of waste in all its forms.

The two boxes to the left represent human issues and the two in the middle hardware. The two above the central line are about doing the right things, the two below are about doing things right.

So a piece of equipment operating incorrectly, say a leaking compressed air line, goes under 'maintenance', whereas if you do not have the correct size of air lines, then that comes under 'equipment'. Taking the example further, specifying the air pressure higher than it needs to be would come under 'procedures'; messing about with compressed air guns comes under 'staff'.

If you run a simple business (for example a small service sector operation), you could probably do one diagram for the whole business. For manufacturing, you will probably have to break your operations down into chunks (for example boilers, fleet, moulding process, coatings, goods out and so on).

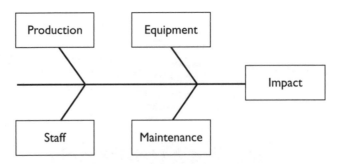

Figure A3.1 Terra Infirma brainstorming tool

The standard process is:

- Draw each diagram big – very big.
- Arm your team with a load of post-its: one colour for problems and one for solutions.
- Get the team to put their ideas on post-its and stick them on the diagrams.
- Brainstorm solutions for the problems: put them on post-its too.
- Filter all the solutions by placing them on a graph with axes of 'ease of implementation' and 'effectiveness once implemented'.

This will give you a prioritized action plan where the high priority actions are the easy to implement/very effective solutions.

Notes

1   Facts taken from the WWF One Planet Living Campaign: www.wwf.org.uk/oneplanet/ophome.asp.

2   Porritt, J. (2006) *Capitalism As If The World Matters*, Earthscan, London.

3   WCED (1987) *Our Common Future*, World Commission on Environment and Development, Oxford, aka The Brundtland Report.

4   O'Riordan, T. and Cameron, J. (1994) *Interpreting the Precautionary Principle*, Earthscan, London.

5   Jackson, T. (1996) *Material Concerns: Pollution, Profit and Quality of Life*, Routledge, London.

6   DEFRA (2006) 'Evaluation of the energy efficiency commitment 2002–05', www.defra.gov.uk/environment/climatechange/uk/household/supplier/pdf/eec-evaluation.pdf, last accessed 7 September 2009.

7   Quoted from the Department of Trade & Industry website, www.dti.gov.uk, last accessed 7 September 2009.

8   www.greenmarketing.com, last accessed 7 September 2009.

9   www.beermat.biz, last accessed 7 September 2009.

10   www.businesslink.gov.uk, last accessed 7 September 2009.

11   von Weizsäcker, E., Lovins, A. B. and Lovins, L. H. (1997) *Factor Four: Doubling Wealth, Halving Resource Use*, Earthscan, London.

12   www.factor10-institute.org, last accessed 7 September 2009.

13   www.naturalstep.org, last accessed 7 September 2009.

14   www.biothinking.com, last accessed 7 September 2009.

15   www.mbdc.com, last accessed 7 September 2009.

16   http://news.bbc.co.uk/1/hi/sci/tech/5406458.stm, last accessed 7 September 2009.

17   Walker, P. (2006) *Change Management for Sustainable Development*, IEMA Best Practice Series.

18   See www.computing.co.uk/business-green/news/2201847/green-
      initiatives-deliver or www.guardian.co.uk/money/2003/sep/12/
      ethicalmoney.workandcareers, last accessed 7 September 2009.

19   Ashley Lodge, Harper Collins, speaking at the Low Carbon Innovation
      Exchange, London, 26 June 2008.

20   www.woking.gov.uk/council/planning/publications/climateneutral2/
      energy.pdf, last accessed 7 September 2009.

21   www.envirowise.org.uk, last accessed 7 September 2009.

22   Ehrenfeld, J. (2008) *Sustainability by Design*, Yale University Press, New
      Haven, CT.

23   www.ghgprotocol.org, last accessed 7 September 2009.

24   www.sdu.nhs.uk/downloads/draft_nhs_carbon_reduction_strategy.pdf,
      last accessed 7 September 2009.

25   www.defra.gov.uk/environment/business/envrp/pdf/conversion-factors.pdf,
      last accessed 7 September 2009.

26   For example: www.aecb.net/forum/index.php?topic=1064.0, last accessed
      7 September 2009.

27   See www.pre.nl/eco-indicator95/eco-indicator95.htm for more details,
      last accessed 7 September 2009.

28   Quist, J. and Vregragt, P. J. (2003) 'Backcasting for Industrial
      Transformations and Systems Innovations Towards Sustainability:
      Relevance for Governance?', proceedings of the 2003 Berlin Conference
      on the Human Dimensions of Global Environmental Change.

29   Robinson, J. (1982) 'Energy backcasting: A proposed method of policy
      analysis', *Energy Policy*, vol 10, no 4, pp337–344.

30   Adapted from Bannister, D. and Hickman, R. (2005) 'Looking over the
      horizon: Visioning and backcasting for UK transport policy', Department
      of Transport, 2004/2005.

31   Thompson, M., Ellis, R. and Widavsky, A. (1990) *Cultural Theory*,
      Westview, Boulder, CO.

32   DETR (1995): 'A guide to risk assessment and risk management for
      environmental protection', Department of the Environment, Transport
      and the Regions.

33   www.guardian.co.uk/news/2003/oct/16/wrap.janeperrone, last accessed
     7 September 2009.

34   www.worldwildlife.org/what/partners/corporate/Coke/item6664.html,
     last accessed 7 September 2009.

35   Adapted from Hockerts, K. (2002) *SustainNovation! Analysing the
     Development of Sustainability Innovations*, Towards Sustainable Products
     Conference, BSI, Chiswick, London, October 2002.

36   DEFRA (2006) 'Evaluation of the energy efficiency commitment
     2002–05', www.defra.gov.uk/environment/climatechange/uk/household/
     supplier/pdf/eec-evaluation.pdf, last accessed 7 September 2009.

37   www.rmi.org/images/PDFs/Transportation/T07–01_DustToDust.pdf,
     last accessed 7 September 2009.

38   www.asa.org.uk/asa/adjudications/non_broadcast/Adjudication+Details.
     htm?Adjudication_id=43476, last accessed 7 September 2009.

39   http://news.bbc.co.uk/1/hi/business/6903302.stm, last accessed
     7 September 2009.

40   www.forecourttrader.co.uk/news/fullstory.php/aid/1843/Detect_to__
     protect.html, last accessed 7 September 2009.

41   The Wikipedia entry for HAZOP is very useful:
     http://en.wikipedia.org/wiki/Hazop, last accessed 7 September 2009.

42   Envirowise 2008, 'EN506 Recycle waste and cut costs to the
     environment', www.envirowise.gov.uk/uk/Our-Services/Publications/
     EN506-Recycle-waste-and-cut-costs-to-the-environment.html, last
     accessed 7 September 2009.

43   www.egger.com/pdf/BR_Environment-Sustainability_EPDs_EN.pdf, last
     accessed 7 September 2009.

44   www.wasteawareconstruction.org.uk/colour.asp, last accessed
     7 September 2009.

45   www.morethanwaste.com/Site/Default.aspx/855669C537E62797CEAB,
     last accessed 7 September 2009.

46   For more information on degree days from the Carbon Trust:
     www.carbontrust.co.uk/resource/degree_days/what_are.htm, last accessed
     7 September 2009.

47   www.lowcarbonlife.net/default.asp?page=41, last accessed 7 September 2009.

48   www.envirowise.gov.uk/uk/Topics-and-Issues/Water/Useful-Facts-and-Figures.html, last accessed 7 September 2009.

49   DEFRA (2008) '2008 Guidelines to Defra's GHG Conversion Factors: Methodology Paper for Transport Emission Factors', July 2008, www.defra.gov.uk/environment/business/envrp/pdf/passenger-transport.pdf, last accessed 7 September 2009.

50   www.dft.gov.uk/pgr/sustainable/travelplans/work, last accessed 7 September 2009.

51   www.dft.gov.uk/pgr/sustainable/teleworking, last accessed 7 September 2009.

52   Goodhall, C. (2007) *How To Live A Low Carbon Life*, Earthscan, London.

53   www.monbiot.com/archives/2006/10/19/selling-indulgences, last accessed 7 September 2009.

54   Jackson, T. (1996) *Material Concerns: Pollution, Profit and Quality of Life*, Routledge, London.

55   For more information, see the Process Intensification Network: www.pinetwork.org, last accessed 7 September 2009.

56   Monbiot, G. (2006) *Heat: How To Stop The Planet Burning*, Penguin Press, London.

57   http://news.bbc.co.uk/1/hi/sci/tech/5406458.stm, last accessed 7 September 2009.

58   Anderson, J., Shiers, D. and Sinclair, M. (2002) *The Green Guide to Specification*, 3rd Edition, Blackwell Science Ltd, Oxford, UK.

59   Sustaine (2002) 'Building-in sustainability: A guide to sustainable construction and development in the North East', Sustainability North East/Durham County Council.

60   National Water Demand Management Centre, Environment Agency (2000) 'A Study of Domestic Greywater Recycling'.

61   www.ciwmb.ca.gov/greenbuilding/Design/CostBenefit/ExecSummary.pdf, last accessed 7 September 2009.

62   www.symbiosis.dk, last accessed 7 September 2009.

63   www.nisp.org.uk/what_is.aspx, last accessed 7 September 2009.

64 Neremow, N. L. (1995) *Zero Pollution for Industry: Waste Minimization Through Industrial Complexes*, John Wiley & Sons, Chichester.
65 Benyus, J. M. (1996) *Biomimicry*, Perennial, New York.
66 Savransky, S. D. (2000): *Engineering of Creativity: Introduction to TRIZ Methodology of Inventive Problem Solving*, CRC Press, Boca Raton, FL.

Index